Praise for *Irrevocable*

"This book is a powerful witness to the vital significance of the divine name for the Christian tradition, showing how its rediscovery may serve as a linchpin in overcoming Christianity's deep-seated Israel-forgetfulness. Soulen's retrieval is of fundamental doctrinal import, with far-reaching ramifications for the structure of Christian thought, not only in relation to the problem of supersessionism, but also in relation to the grammar of its doctrine of God."

—Susannah Ticciati, King's College London

"Kendall Soulen's *Irrevocable* is a profound series of insights on what it means, first for Judaism and then for Christianity, to affirm that the God of Israel has a personal identity designated by a proper name. This enables both Christians and Jews to honestly speak of worshipping the same God, albeit with some significant differences, and not merging into an incoherent syncretism or dissolving into a vapid, post-religious universalism."

—David Novak, University of Toronto

"Soulen makes a strong and timely case for the necessity of the Tetragrammaton in Christian theological language to identify the true God, who is the God of both biblical Testaments. This is a significant post-supersessionist theology that navigates how we read both Testaments freshly."

—Gavin D'Costa, University of Bristol

"Israel is *the* conundrum for Christians, and Kendall Soulen's work these past thirty years has consistently addressed it with seriousness, precision, and creativity. *Irrevocable* is an important new contribution to that work, especially in its treatment of how consideration of the divine name can move Christians toward better thinking about Israel."
—Paul Griffiths, author of *Regret: A Theology* and *Why Read Pascal?*

"Soulen has not only thought deeply about Judaism and the divine name YHWH; he has done this in the context of a wonderfully stimulating and erudite engagement with the full range of Christian dogmatic loci. The result is a theology that is post-supersessionist in the best sense—that is, not by jettisoning core Christian beliefs, but by seeking to articulate these beliefs ever more rigorously, devoutly, and generously. Whether agreeing or disagreeing, all will benefit from learning to think with Soulen."
—Matthew Levering, Mundelein Seminary

"*Irrevocable* is a concise statement of the case for why Christian theology, in its Trinitarianism most of all, should 'orbit the unspoken Tetragrammaton.' Soulen's project has always been stimulating and provocative, but here he has refined and reformulated his arguments to make them more incisive, more constructive, and more immediately useful for theologians from many traditions. This book has helped me to theologize more faithfully, and even to read the Bible more accurately."
—Fred Sanders, Biola University

Irrevocable

Irrevocable

*The Name of God and the Unity
of the Christian Bible*

R. Kendall Soulen

Fortress Press
Minneapolis

A previous treatment of the topic of chapter 1 by this author was published
as "The Standard Canonical Narrative and the Problem of Supersessionism,"
in *Introduction to Messianic Judaism*, ed. David Rudolph and Joel Willitts (Grand
Rapids, MI: Zondervan, 2013).

A previous treatment of the topic of chapter 2 by this author was published as
"Hallowed Be Thy Name: The Tetragrammaton and the Name of the Trinity," in
Jews and Christians: People of God, ed. Robert W. Jenson and Carl Braaten (Grand
Rapids, MI: Eerdmans, 2003).

Chapter 3 is adapted from "The Name above Every Name: The Eternal Identity of the Second Person of the Trinity and the Covenant of Grace," in *Advancing Trinitarian Doctrine: Explorations in Constructive Dogmatics*, ed. Oliver D. Crips and Fred Sanders (Grand Rapids, MI: Zondervan, 2014).

Chapter 5 is adapted from "Jesus and the Divine Name," in "Festschrift for Christopher Morse," special issue, *Union Seminary Quarterly Review* 65, nos. 1–2 (Spring 2015): 47–58.

Chapter 6 is adapted from "Trinity and Church after Supersessionism: A Thought Experiment with Jenson and Augustine," in *The Promise of Robert W. Jenson's Theology: Constructive Engagements*, ed. Stephen Wright (Minneapolis: Fortress, 2017).

Chapter 7 is adapted from "'They Are Israelites': The Priority of the Present Tense for Jewish-Christian Relations," in *Between Gospel and Election: Explorations in the Interpretation of Romans 9–11*, ed. Ross Wagner and Florian Wilk, Wissenschaftliche Untersuchungen zum Neuen Testament (Tübingen, Germany: Mohr Siebeck, 2010).

Chapter 8 is adapted from "The Sign of Jonah: A Christian Perspective on the Relation of the Abrahamic Faiths," in *Crisis, Call, and Leadership in the Abrahamic Traditions*, ed. Peter Ochs and William Stacy Johnson (New York: Palgrave Macmillan, 2009).

Chapter 9 is adapted from "Go Tell Pharaoh: Or, Why Empires Prefer a Nameless God," *Cultural Encounters: A Journal for the Theology of Culture* 1, no. 2 (Summer 2005): 49–60; reprinted in Jürgen Moltmann, Timothy R. Eberhart, and Matthew W. Charlton, eds., *The Economy of Salvation: Festschrift for M. Douglas Meeks* (Eugene, OR: Wipf and Stock, 2015).

Cover image: Kristin Miller
Cover design: Kristin Miller

Paperback ISBN: 979-8-8898-3630-8
Hardcover ISBN: 978-1-5064-8118-0
eBook ISBN: 978-1-5064-8119-7

For Hans Frei and Michael Wyschogrod

CONTENTS

INTRODUCTION

HALF THE WORLD'S Christians belong to churches that have recently affirmed that God's election of the Jewish people is "irrevocable." The churches' belated endorsement of a conclusion that the apostle Paul reached two millennia ago represents a seismic shift from the Christian past. It also presents Christians today with a major challenge: showing how their new understanding of one part of the Bible coheres with their customary understanding of the rest of it. The second-century theologian Irenaeus famously compared the Bible to a mosaic whose pieces can be arranged in different ways. Properly arranged, the mosaic reveals the image of a king, but arranged according to gnostic preference, it shows a fox. The challenge for Christians is to show that their affirmation of God's irrevocable election of the Jewish people is an enhancement of the biblical mosaic rather than a well-intentioned but slipshod intervention that mars its evangelical design.

This book argues that a key for meeting this challenge is paying attention to the Bible's single most important and most neglected and misunderstood word: the Tetragrammaton, the traditionally unspoken personal proper name of God. Irenaeus himself was ignorant of the Tetragrammaton, like most Christians of the patristic era. It is partly for this reason, I think, that his influential account of the Bible's unity was marred by the distortion of supersessionism. This book demonstrates the difference the Tetragrammaton makes for how Christians understand the theological unity of the Bible. Doing justice to the Bible's pancanonical witness to God's proper name, I argue, can help Christians show that an Irenaean account of the Bible's unity is fully compatible with the church's affirmation of God's irrevocable election of the Jewish people. In fact, restoring the Tetragrammaton to its rightful place

1

in the mosaic's design removes some fox-like features that don't properly belong to it and enhances its portrait of the king.

Most of the chapters in this book have been previously published, but I have revised them extensively and substantively for the purposes of this volume. They therefore appear here with new titles so that they are not confused with their antecedents. An exception is chapter 4 ("Why Did God Choose the Jews?"), which I wrote for this book and which is published here for the first time. Two chapters appear with their original titles because they differ only in minor ways from their previously published versions. They are chapter 7 ("'They Are Israelites': The Priority of the Present Tense for Jewish-Christian Relations") and chapter 8 ("The Sign of Jonah: A Christian Perspective on the Relation of the Abrahamic Faiths"). Finally, chapter 9 appears with its original title even though I rewrote it extensively for this book ("'Go Tell Pharaoh': Or Why Empires Prefer a Nameless God"). I kept the original title because I liked it too much to change.

Richard N. Soulen, my father and trusted adviser on theological matters (and what is not a theological matter?), improved the book with a sharp editorial eye. I am grateful to Carey Newman of Fortress Press for his enthusiastic support of this project and his contributions to it. Two departed mentors have been frequently on my mind as I have worked on this book. Hans Frei sparked my love for dogmatic theology and taught me by example that the most interesting way to do it was as an exercise in the theological interpretation of the Bible. Michael Wyschogrod helped me realize that the distinction between Jew and gentile is one of the Bible's most mysteriously beautiful features and a sign, instrument, and foretaste of the world to come. This book is dedicated to the memory of Hans and Michael with deep affection and gratitude.

Scripture, Trinity, Election

SCRIPTURE

THE UNITY OF THE BIBLE AND THE PROBLEM OF SUPERSESSIONISM

SUPERSESSIONISM IS NOT an attractive word, but it can be a useful one if it is clearly defined. In this book, *supersessionism* labels what some Christian communions have come to identify as an error in Christian teaching, in a manner similar to other theological isms such as modalism, subordinationism, and so on. In this case, the error is the belief that the Jews are no longer God's elect people. The rationales that Christians have given in support of this belief have varied. The two most common are that God's covenant with the Jewish people is obsolete and/or that the Jews forfeited it. But whatever its accompanying rationale, the essence of supersessionism remains the same. It is the Christian belief that the Jews are no longer what they once were—God's elect people.

The conviction that supersessionism so defined is an *error* is relatively novel. Until recently, many if not most Christians took it for granted that the Jews were no longer God's chosen people. While the belief was not a dogma or doctrine in the formal sense, it fit so neatly with beliefs that were dogmas and doctrines that its truth seemed obvious. In 1964 and 1965, however, the Second Vatican Council of the Roman Catholic Church issued authoritative statements declaring that the covenant God made with the Jews was "irrevocable," for God does not go back on his promises. Since then, many other Christian communions have issued teaching documents that affirm the same thing.[1] As evidence, these statements almost always cite chapters 9–11 of Paul's Letter to the Romans. This is the New Testament passage that addresses the covenantal status of the Jewish people after Christ at the greatest length and in the most explicit terms. Paul begins the section by using a present tense form of the verb *to be* to affirm that Jews who have not believed the gospel "*are* Israelites" and that "to them belong the adoption, the glory, the covenants, the giving of the law, the worship, and the promises" (Rom 9:4). At the close of the section, and after many twists and turns, Paul returns to his starting point and reaffirms it with words of crystal clarity: "As regards election they are beloved, for the sake of their ancestors; for the gifts and calling of God are irrevocable" (Rom 11:28–29).

God's irrevocable election of the Jewish people is the affirmation, the contradiction of which is supersessionism.[2] The fact that this affirmation has been publicly endorsed by Christian communions representing well over a billion Christians is one of truly historic significance. Since the close of the apostolic era, corporate Christian teaching on a comparably important matter has seldom changed so radically over such a relatively short span of time. The change lays a new foundation for the relationship between Christians and Jews, one whose full theological and practical implications are likely to take generations to discern.

One implication, however, is already clear: the church's rejection of supersessionism confronts it with a major hermeneutical challenge. Christians in the past who believed that the church had replaced the Jews as God's people did so because they saw this belief as an integral part of a comprehensive reading of the Bible, one that Christians still employ today. To discover that a key feature of this reading is mistaken is no small thing. The discovery requires Christians to examine how their customary reading of the Bible harbored the error of supersessionism, and how that reading can be reenvisioned so that God's irrevocable election of the Jews appears as a cogent part of the Bible's comprehensive witness to Jesus Christ. A concept that is helpful in addressing these questions is that of a canonical narrative.

The Idea of a Canonical Narrative

The idea of a canonical narrative rests on the insight that interpreting a complex text such as the Bible requires one to move back and forth between smaller and larger units of meaning. To understand the sentence "The gifts and the calling of God are irrevocable" (Rom 11:29), one must understand the individual words that make it up. But the opposite is also true. To understand any single word in that sentence, one must make a judgment about the meaning of the sentence as a whole, for a sentence is not just a string of words but a semantic unit in its own right that determines the meaning of words according to rules of grammar and syntax. A similar relationship between part and whole repeats itself at ever-larger levels of literary organization. To understand Romans 9–11, for example, one must make a host of judgments about the sentences that make up the passage and the rhetorical units in which they appear. But one must also venture a judgment about how the passage fits in Paul's letter as a whole, for the total composition of the letter governs how its different sections function.

At the highest level of literary organization, making sense of any passage in the Christian canon requires one to venture a judgment about the meaning of the canon as a whole. It is true that not everyone thinks this last step is valid. The canon differs from Paul's Letter to the Romans because the canon is not the product of a single human author but a sprawling anthology of documents created by many people in varied circumstances over a long stretch of time. Many contemporary biblical scholars are so impressed by the Bible's diversity that they passionately resist the suggestion that it can be meaningfully interpreted as a unity. The best that can be done, they maintain, is to understand the Bible's components singly and on their own terms, without attempting to understand them as contributing to or participating in a deeper unity.

Attention to the canon's internal variety, so characteristic of modern biblical studies, has yielded many benefits, much as ever-stronger microscopes yield sharper images of a single stone or ceramic tile. Yet such a focus by itself is incomplete when measured by the interpretive practices of the communities that created the biblical canons in the first place—namely, Israel and the church. True, the individual parts of the Christian canon have no single human author. Still, the Christian canon as a whole does: the church. Moreover, the church gathered and defined the canon based on the conviction that this collection of writings, beginning with Israel's holy books, is the privileged written instrument used by the Holy Spirit to instruct the church in the things of God. Christians have traditionally interpreted the canon as a theological unity, even though its parts have no single human author, on the supposition that the unity of its parts is underwritten by the oneness of the God that it attests. I believe that this supposition is a necessary concomitant of the church's life and that the ever-renewed effort to understand the canon as a theological unity is imperative for the church in every age.

It is at this juncture that the concept of a canonical construal or a canonical narrative proves useful.[3] A canonical narrative is an interpretive framework for understanding the Bible as a literary and theological unity. A canonical narrative is not the same as the Bible itself. Rather, it is a working hypothesis about how the canon hangs together as a coherent witness to and instrument of God. A canonical narrative comprises countless many decisions about the meaning of individual words, sentences, rhetorical units, books, and so on, but it is more than just the sum of all such decisions. Just as bread is not simply certain quantities of flour, salt, oil, and yeast but the product of their interaction, so the Bible interpreted by means of a canonical narrative is not merely the sum of countless decisions about the meaning of its parts. As Charles Wood observes, "It is the new instrument produced by the working together of these parts when they are taken in a certain way, that is, according to the canonical construal which has been adopted."[4]

The Standard Canonical Narrative ...

At first glance, the concept of a canonical narrative might seem to introduce an intolerable degree of relativism into biblical interpretation by multiplying the possible grounds of disagreement ad infinitum. In fact, the concept points to a powerfully stabilizing factor in Christian tradition. Interpreters who share a common canonical narrative can disagree about the meaning of individual passages while still agreeing on the larger story of which they are a part. They are like artisans who differ about where to place a single stone in a mosaic while agreeing on the overall design. Irenaeus of Lyon compared the Bible conceived as a theological unity to a beautiful mosaic composed of precious stones that skillfully portrays the image of a king. (Gnostics, he charged, were like those who rearranged the pieces into the image of a fox, and a badly executed fox at that.)[5]

In fact, the construal of the Bible's unity that eventually became customary among Christians was first articulated in detail by Irenaeus himself. The standard canonical narrative that he bequeathed to subsequent generations can be characterized by the answers it gives to four key questions about the "design" that the Bible displays when properly apprehended as a theological and literary unity:

Q. What is the canon's overarching plot?

A. Creation, fall, redemption in Jesus Christ, and final consummation. Like the synopsis of a play or opera, these four episodes constitute the narrative "foreground" that encompasses all other biblical and extrabiblical reality.

Q. What is the canon's hermeneutical center?

A. Jesus Christ, God's eternal Word made flesh. While the Holy Spirit enables the canon to refer to Jesus Christ in a vast variety of ways, he is the ultimate focal point that gives unity and coherence to the diversity of the scriptural witness.

Q. How are the Old and New Testaments related?

A. They are parts of a single economy of salvation centered on the incarnation of God's eternal Word and the outpouring of the Spirit. The Old Testament anticipates these events in a prophetic, preparatory, and typological way, while the New Testament testifies to them in an apostolic, definitive, and archetypical way. In Irenaeus's influential formulation, the Testaments have the same substance and differ only in their outer form.[6]

A final question is especially important because its answer integrates the other three and gives them a foundation in the eternal identity of God:

Q. Who is the God attested by the canon as a whole?

A. The Holy Trinity—the Father, the Son, and the Holy Spirit. The Trinity (1) creates, redeems, and consummates; (2) orders the economy of salvation in the two dispensations of the old and new covenants; and (3) restores humankind to fellowship with the Father through the incarnation of the Son and outpouring of the Holy Spirit, a work that will be completed with the consummation of the age and the dawn of the world to come.

Though forged almost two millennia ago, this canonical narrative remains familiar to most Christians today. They, like Christians of the past, absorb at least its main rudiments in proportion to their participation in Christian worship, devotion, catechesis, and so on.

... And the Problem of Supersessionism

Christians today are commonly aware of various challenges that have arisen over time that contest the viability of the standard model as a truthful and fitting description of reality. Some of these challenges have a *formal* character—that is, they are indifferent to the contents of Christian belief but represent a broad shift in cultural perspective that nevertheless erodes the model's overall coherence. An example is the rise of historical consciousness, which views the Bible as a record of the past to be fitted into a critical understanding of human history like any other ancient document. (This shift in perspective characterizes modern biblical studies and underwrites its focus on the Bible's internal diversity.)[7] Other challenges have a more material character—that is, they target prominent features of the Bible itself and the hermeneutical model that purports to unify it. The nineteenth-century abolitionist Matilda Joslyn Gage voiced such a material criticism when she charged, "All the evils that have resulted from dignifying one sex and degrading the other may be traced to this central error: a belief in a trinity of masculine Gods in One, from which the feminine element is wholly eliminated."[8]

The fact that the contemporary church has identified supersessionism as an *error* poses a challenge of the second, more material kind. Without too much distortion, we can formulate the judgment that underlies the church's rejection of supersessionism this way: "All the evils that have resulted from dignifying the church and degrading the Jewish people may be traced to this central error: a belief that the Jews are no longer the elect people of God."[9] Just as Gage's criticism challenges Christians to learn to read the Bible in a nonpatriarchal way, so the church's affirmation of Israel's irrevocable election challenges Christians to learn to read the Bible in a nonsupersessionist way. That is hard to do, however, because the church's customary reading of the Bible suggests powerful rationales for believing that God's covenant with the Jews is a thing of the past.

One such rationale is the belief that God abrogated God's covenant with the Jews on account of their sins. When this rationale undergirds the idea that the Jews are no longer God's people, we can call the belief *punitive* supersessionism. The mosaic tiles that have prompted Christians to endorse punitive supersessionism are plentiful and sharply edged. They include the many biblical passages in both the Old and New Testaments that direct fierce prophetic criticism against Israel and threaten her with exile, rejection, and destruction. Punitive supersessionism merely assumes that God at last made good on these threats because the Word "came to what was his own, and his own people did not accept him" (John 1:11). Because the Jews rejected Jesus, God in turn rejected the Jews, and thus they are no longer God's people.

Another rationale that can undergird the belief that the Jews are no longer God's people is the idea that God made a covenant with them for the exclusive purpose of preparing for Christ's advent, after which God's covenant with the Jewish people naturally and fittingly expired. We can call this *economic* supersessionism because it concerns Israel's purpose in the economy of salvation. Economic supersessionism is often less overtly polemical than punitive supersessionism, but the rationale that it provides for the belief that the Jews are no longer God's people is just as powerful, if not more so, because it grounds the belief in what God positively intends rather than what God negatively rejects. God always intended for Mary to be the last Jewish mother and for Jesus to be the last Jew—or, at any rate, for the apostles to be the last Jews. This idea gains plausibility from the fact that it reflects and extends a prominent feature of the standard canonical narrative's basic design—namely, its division of the one economy of salvation into two parts: the old covenant and the new. If the purpose of the old covenant is to prepare for and prefigure the new, and if the purpose of the new is to fulfill and replace the old, then it seems to follow necessarily that God's covenant with the Jews is over. Everything that made it possible for Israel to be a distinct people in the first place—circumcision, membership in Abraham's chosen lineage, the Mosaic law, the temple, and so on—existed solely for the purpose of preparing for Christ and the church. Once Christ and the church arrive, these things lose their raison d'être, as do the people whose existence depended on them. The Jews are no longer God's people because the form of their covenant with God expired long ago; it is obsolete, just as Jews themselves are if they stubbornly insist on living as Jews past their "expiration date."

These two rationales, in turn, promote a third feature of the standard canonical narrative as it is commonly envisioned—namely, its "Israel-forgetfulness." Israel-forgetfulness is not a third rationale for supersessionism but a hermeneutical consequence that flows from the other two.[10] It refers to the fact that when we step back and look at the design of the standard model at the largest scale, we do not have to pay attention to God's covenant with Israel at all. Our attention is drawn rather to the plot sequence that defines its main contours: creation, fall, redemption in Christ, and final consummation. This, it seems, provides a sufficient basis for theological reflection by itself, while the bulk of the Hebrew Scriptures can recede from our attention without much loss. To be sure, we *can* develop doctrines such as the Trinity, creation, anthropology, hamartiology, Christology, ecclesiology, and eschatology with reference to Genesis 4 through Malachi. But we don't have to. As a matter of fact, Christians prior to the modern period frequently did quarry all of the Old Testament at length and in detail, often with brilliant results. Still, they generally did so for the purpose of showing how it prefigured the New Testament. In more recent times, Christians have often dispensed with this labor and have nevertheless arrived at doctrinal conclusions that stand in strong continuity with the premodern past. This is possible because the bulk of the Old Testament was rarely decisive for shaping doctrinal conclusions in the first place, which much rather rested primarily on the model's foreground plot. For this reason too, Christian theology has traditionally lacked a doctrinal locus devoted to developing the contents of Genesis 4 to Malachi.

These three features of the standard canonical narrative as traditionally conceived give it a decidedly supersessionist cast. If we think of the standard model as a mosaic and God's covenant with Israel as a certain kind of stone with a distinctive range of colors, then Israel-forgetfulness is the absence of these stones from the mosaic's most prominent design, economic supersessionism is their incorporation into an intricate pattern of divine providence that abruptly comes to an end after the incarnation, and punitive supersessionism is the fact that the stones are not particularly attractive in the first place. Setting the metaphor aside, we can say that the three features have been mutually reinforcing. Economic and punitive supersessionism feed Israel-forgetfulness by providing the reasons Israel can be safely forgotten, and the apparent self-sufficiency of the design that remains reinforces the belief that economic and punitive supersessionism must be true.

The Tetragrammaton and the Standard Canonical Narrative

If this analysis of the standard canonical narrative is roughly correct, then we can see why the contemporary church's rejection of supersessionism poses a serious hermeneutical challenge. The problem is to show how removing supersessionism from the standard model is something other than a well-intentioned but slipshod intervention that spoils its overall portrait of a king.

One possible response to the challenge is to say that it can't be met. That is what I claimed in *The God of Israel and Christian Theology*. In that book, I called for "a renewed conversion of basic Christian forms of thought toward the God of Israel."[11] I maintained that to accomplish this conversion, Christians need to replace the standard canonical narrative with a new canonical narrative that is more translucent to God's identity as the God of Israel, the God who doesn't go back on God's promises to the Jews or anyone else. I believe more strongly than ever that Christians need to find a way to read the Bible that is transparent to God's identity as the faithful God of Israel. In the meantime, though, I have changed my mind about a couple of other things.

For one thing, I no longer think that the new canonical narrative that I proposed is an acceptable alternative to the standard canonical narrative. I do think that my proposal successfully identified two features of the Bible that any canonical construal must do justice to if it is to avoid the error of supersessionism. They are the Bible's pancanonical witness to (1) God's irrevocable election of the Jewish people and (2) the unerasable distinction between Israel and the nations that results from it. I also think that I was on the right track in arguing that the distinction between Jew and gentile is a "sign, instrument, and foretaste" (Lesslie Newbigin) of God's eschatological blessing and one of the most mysteriously beautiful features of the Christian Bible.[12] Unfortunately, my alternative canonical narrative failed on a different front. It did not make clear that when Christians convert more fully to the God of Israel, they also convert more fully to the Holy Trinity revealed in Christ. In fact, my construal suggested (though it certainly did not intend) the opposite: one conversion comes at the cost of the other.

For another thing, my estimate of the nonsupersessionist potential of the standard canonical narrative has changed. I no longer think that it is *necessarily* supersessionist. In my earlier book, I compared supersessionism to a flaw in the heart of a crystal, the crystal being the standard canonical narrative. But the church's customary reading of the Bible is not as rigid as that. Irenaeus's image of a mosaic is better. The tiles of a mosaic can be arranged in a multitude of ways that all exhibit the same basic design. If a particular arrangement is flawed in some way, the tiles can be rearranged so that the flaw is removed but the basic design is preserved. That is how I now think of the relationship between the standard canonical narrative and the error of supersessionism. Christians are accustomed to seeing its design executed in a way that incorporates the error of supersessionism. But with time and labor, they can rearrange the model's tiles in a way that removes supersessionism without spoiling the basic design and, in fact, makes its portrait of a king more beautiful than before. To put it another way, I now believe that there is a way to envision the standard canonical narrative that shows that converting more fully to the God of Israel and converting more fully to the triune God revealed in Christ are one and the same.

The only way to make a fully convincing case for that claim would be to flesh out the standard canonical narrative in a fully orbed, nonsupersessionist way. This book falls far short of meeting that challenge, though I do hope to meet it more fully in a future publication.[13] What the present book offers is a series of more fragmentary studies that contribute to that end. The chapters examine specific regions of the mosaic, as it were, where crucial decisions must be made if Irenaeus's design is to be restored in a nonsupersessionist way. The chapters address the following questions: How do we most appropriately name the Holy Trinity? How should we think about the Trinity's eternal election of grace in Jesus Christ? Why did God choose the Jews? Does Jesus's fulfillment of Jewish ceremonial practice always entail its obsolescence? What is the nature of the church? And, how does Romans 9–11 bear on relations between Christians and Jews? The book's last two chapters are less directly concerned with the design of the standard model but attempt to show how a broadly nonsupersessionist perspective bears on other topics of contemporary concern—specifically, Christianity's relation to Islam and recent proposals that advocate a "pluralist" understanding of religions.

The golden thread that runs through all the chapters is the attention they pay to a single word: the Tetragrammaton, the four-lettered Hebrew name that is traditionally represented in English translations of the Bible in small caps as LORD. Despite the familiarity of its printed surrogate, I do not think that Christian theology has yet succeeded in taking the full measure of the significance of the Tetragrammaton for the unity of the Christian canon. Irenaeus himself was completely unaware of it, and although the situation has improved since his day, a surprising amount of the original deficit remains. I think that failure to do justice to the Tetragrammaton's significance lies at the root of the fact that the standard model has traditionally "skewed supersessionist" and that it has inevitably created other problems for Christian theology too. Conversely, I think that the most important step that Christians can take to give the standard model a more natural, nonsupersessionist shape is to attend carefully to the pancanonical witness to the Tetragrammaton and the God who bears it. Doing so, I believe, is *the* key to showing that, for Christians, converting more fully to the God of Israel and converting more fully to the triune God revealed in Christ are the same thing.

Giving plausibility to such expansive claims on behalf of a single word is the task of the chapters ahead. Still, two brief considerations may help dispel an initial appearance of sheer implausibility. The Tetragrammaton is indeed only a single word, but it is arguably the single most *important* word in the Bible, for the simple reason that it is the proper name of the biblically attested God. We use proper names for nonfungible objects: objects for which qualitative duplicates would be unacceptable. The biblically attested God is such a nonfungible "object." The importance of the Tetragrammaton is that it expresses God's nonfungibility in a way that precedes, unifies, and illuminates all the other divine names in the Bible—including the name "Jesus." If the Christian canon has literary and theological unity at all, it is because of the unity of the God who bears this name, and it can be adequately discerned only in light of this name and the God it identifies. Second, while the Tetragrammaton is not the Bible's most frequently attested *word*, it is the Bible's most frequently attested *proper name* (in second place is *Israel*). The Tetragrammaton occurs almost seven thousand times in the Old Testament—or, on average, about seven times per chapter—and it occurs with roughly similar frequency in the New Testament, albeit always by means of oblique allusions of which *Lord* (*kyrios*) is but one (more on that in subsequent chapters). Taken together, these considerations suggest what is apt to go wrong with a construal of the Bible's unity that doesn't do justice to the Tetragrammaton. It is like executing a mosaic while leaving a vast pile of the most precious stones on the shop floor.

To conclude this chapter and anticipate the ones ahead, I will revisit the four marks that characterize the basic design of the standard canonical narrative and briefly indicate how attending to the Bible's pancanonical witness to the Tetragrammaton can reshape our understanding of it:

Q. Who is the God attested by the canon as a whole?

A. *The Holy Trinity: the Father, the Son, and the Holy Spirit.* This answer is correct but incomplete. Behind the standard model's "Israel-forgetfulness" lurks a deeper amnesia: *forgetfulness of the Tetragrammaton.*[14] Christians have generally recognized that they can specify the Trinity's eternal identity and mystery only if they supplement the baptismal triad with further triads such as "God, Word, Gift"; "Lover, Beloved, Love"; and so on. (This is part of the answer to Gage's criticism, as feminist theologians such as Elizabeth A. Johnson have shown.) What Christians have not commonly understood is that even these two patterns of naming the Trinity remain insufficient in the absence of the Tetragrammaton, a name that (I will argue) belongs eternally to each of the Trinitarian persons in a different way. Restoring the Tetragrammaton to its rightful place in the Bible's witness to the eternal Trinity adjusts the keystone of the standard canonical narrative in a way that has cascading effects for the model as a whole, allowing it to assume a sturdier and nonsupersessionist shape.

Q. What is the canon's overarching plot?

A. *Creation, fall, redemption in Jesus Christ, and final consummation.* There is nothing intrinsically wrong with this answer.
   It becomes problematic only when this foreground narrative
   ceases to be illuminated from the Old Testament's mysterious depths. Remembering the Tetragrammaton prohib-
   its a fracturing of the canon along these lines. The Divine
   Name identifies the God who creates (Gen 2:4–9), redeems
   (Phil 2:9), and consummates (Rev 1:8) in a way that con-
   nects every episode to the God who spoke to Moses at the
   burning bush, the God who caused the nonfungibility of
   God's own name to "rub off" with permanent effect
   on God's people, the Jews.

Q. How are the Old and New Testaments related?

A. *They are parts of a single economy of salvation centered on
   the incarnation of God's eternal Word and the outpouring of the
   Spirit.* Yes, but we cannot properly understand the unity of
   the economy of salvation if we assume (as Christians customarily have) that the New Testament fulfills the Old by
   replacing everything that was characteristic of the economy
   in its distinctively "Old Testament" form. In some cases, the
   New Testament fulfills the Old by *confirming* and *continuing* the Old Testament starting point. An obvious example
   is the Tetragrammaton itself, which the Old Testament introduces as the primordial name of God, and which the New
   Testament confirms as "the name that is above every name"
   (Phil 2:9) at the center of Christian worship. Moreover,
   Jesus and the apostles mark out the Tetragrammaton's special significance in a distinctively Jewish way: they don't
   pronounce it. The practice of reverent nonpronunciation
   is encoded in the literature of the New Testament and has
   subsequently entered the lifeblood of the church—further

evidence that the novelty of the new covenant does not depend on the comprehensive obsolescence of Jewish practice.

Q. What is the canon's hermeneutical center?

A. *Jesus Christ, God's eternal Word made flesh.* Yes, and amen. But the name "Jesus" means "YHWH is Salvation." The two personal proper names can be understood only in light of each other, and of the two, it is the Tetragrammaton that has ontological priority.

The chapters that follow develop these answers in greater detail.

TRINITY

ONE NAME IN THREE INFLECTIONS

All musick is but three parts vied
And multiplied.

—George Herbert, "Easter"

THE DOCTRINE OF the Trinity is the keystone of the church's customary construal of the unity of the Christian canon. It rests on many subordinate judgments about how the parts of the Bible fit together and supports those judgments in turn, giving them a (relatively) stable shape, one whose apex is an "understanding" of the eternal mystery and identity of the God who is revealed in Jesus Christ by the power of the Holy Spirit. An account of the *name* of the Trinity is the sign emblazoned on this keystone, as it were. It is that aspect of a doctrine of the Trinity that concentrates its significance into the briefest possible compass and most concisely exhibits the design that informs the canonical construal as a whole.

So what is the name of the Trinity? Or, given the fact that the Christian tradition has named the Trinity in many ways, what is the *most appropriate* way of naming the Trinity? Contrary to what is often supposed, the Christian tradition has no settled answer to this question. Traditionally, Christian theologians took it for granted that *a* most appropriate way of naming the Trinity was the baptismal triad, "the Father and the Son and the Holy Spirit." But they likewise took it for granted that the eternal identity and mystery of the Trinity could not be adequately illuminated by this "kinship-heavy" triad alone. It was too vulnerable to misunderstanding. To prevent such misunderstanding, it was necessary to name the persons of the Trinity using other triads as well, such as "God, Word, Gift"; "Lover, Beloved, Love"; and so on. In practice, theologians operated as though the *most* appropriate way of naming the Trinity was a blending of the two patterns rather than either pattern by itself.

In recent decades, this tacit consensus has broken down in parts of the church. On the one hand, feminist Christians have charged a male-dominated church with overweighting the baptismal triad, making it the keystone of a patriarchal reading of the Bible that has harmed women and men alike. To counter this, they have argued that no single triad counts as *the* most appropriate way of naming the Trinity. Rather, they maintain the most appropriate way to name the Trinity is to employ an open-ended pattern of naming that uses many different triads drawn from across the range of human experience, of which the baptismal triad is but one among many. Such an approach, they maintain, is true to the insight of apophatic theology that the mystery of the Trinity transcends adequate description by human language and so by any single triad or, indeed, by all possible triads taken together. Other theologians have countered that it belongs to the character of the biblical God to have a determinate identity that can be revealed and cataphatically expressed and that such a revelation has in fact occurred in Jesus Christ. They hold that the baptismal triad is the biblically attested name that best expresses the eternal identity of the Holy Trinity.[1]

One unfortunate by-product of this polarized debate has been its tendency to pit two historically important patterns of naming the Trinity against each other. Another is its implicit suggestion that an emphasis on the Trinity's eternal identity requires a de-emphasis on the Trinity's eternal mystery and vice versa. My own intuition is that part of what bedevils the debate is that it is predicated on an inadequate starting point. The question "What is the most appropriate way of naming the Trinity?" cannot be satisfactorily answered in terms of the two patterns of naming that

Christians have customarily recognized, no matter how the relationship between them is configured. The reason is that neither pattern alone nor both together can take the place of a *third* pattern of naming the Trinity that Christians have commonly left out of the picture altogether. That third pattern of naming the persons of the Trinity orbits a single word: the Tetragrammaton.

The Tetragrammaton is God's final, climactic response to Moses's request for God's name at the burning bush (Exod 3:13–15). To avert a misunderstanding that is extraordinarily widespread among Christians, this climactic name is *not* "I am who I am," which appears in Exodus 3:14. Rather, it is the name that appears in the *following* verse (Exod 3:15), called the Tetragrammaton since ancient times because it consists of four Hebrew characters: *yod*, *he*, *waw*, and *he* (יהוה, YHWH). Christians have long loved to celebrate "I am who I am"; in contrast, for the church's first 1,200 years, most were unaware that the Tetragrammaton existed at all. Oddly enough, what accounts for the postapostolic church's ignorance of the Tetragrammaton is the fact that contemporary Jews held it in uniquely high regard, or more precisely, the fact that Jews expressed their uniquely high regard for this name in a highly particular way: *they didn't pronounce it.* More on that later. For now, the point is that as patristic theologians painstakingly built up a comprehensive reading of the Bible whose keystone was the doctrine of the Trinity, they did so in almost complete ignorance of what Jews (including the writers of the New Testament) regarded as the Bible's single most important word: the Tetragrammaton.[2] Eventually, Christians did become cognizant of the Tetragrammaton, especially in the West, at which point they began to fit it into their understanding of the canon. By that time, however, the church's conception of the Bible's unity had long since taken a supersessionist cast, and Christian interpretations of the Tetragrammaton often followed suit, for example, by conceiving it as the Old Testament *forerunner* of God's "real" name, which was thought to be either "Jesus" or "the Father, the Son, and the Holy Spirit."[3] Modern Bible scholars have also done their part to cement the common Christian assumption that the Tetragrammaton is obsolete by transliterating it as *Yahweh*, a hypothetical reconstruction with no living basis in either Judaism or Christianity.

This helps explain why contemporary Christian debates about the most appropriate way to name the Trinity typically don't take account of the Tetragrammaton. But it does not explain how the Tetragrammaton can possibly provide a way of naming *the Trinity* at all. Since I address that issue in greater detail later in this chapter and in the next, a brief explanation suffices for now. The Tetragrammaton can uniquely identify each of the three persons of the Trinity because each person bears one and the same name *in a different way* that reflects—or better, *constitutes*—their distinctive place in the eternal "economy" of the divine life. The pattern of naming the Trinity that is based on the Tetragrammaton accomplishes with one word what the baptismal triad accomplishes with three and the other pattern of naming accomplishes with an open-ended plurality of triads.

At this point, I can propose the thesis that I want to defend in the rest of this chapter. The most appropriate *way* of naming the Trinity is in fact an ensemble of three *ways*. The three patterns of naming the Trinity are distinct but isomorphic. They use different biblically attested vocabularies to say the same thing in different ways. The patterns are also equally important and interrelated. Each pattern is indispensable for the Bible's witness to the Trinity, but no pattern can do everything, and each depends on the other two to make good its deficiencies and protect it from misunderstanding.

Finally, I want to suggest that each pattern of naming has a special affinity with one person of the Trinity in particular. To highlight this claim, I will call each pattern an *inflection* of the name of the Trinity. According to the *Oxford English Dictionary*, an inflection is "the modification of the form of a word" that expresses "the different grammatical relations into which it may enter"; it is also defined as a "modulation of the voice; in speaking or singing: a change in the pitch or tone of the voice."[4] Bending and blending these definitions, I want to suggest each pattern of naming "inflects" the name of the Trinity in a way that tends to highlight one person and places the other two in its light:

- The pattern of naming that orbits the Tetragrammaton has a special affinity with the first person, the Unoriginate Origin of the divine life. I will therefore dub it the theological inflection of the name of the Trinity.
- The pattern of naming that orbits the baptismal triad has a special affinity with the second person of the Trinity, the only person who "became flesh" (John 1:14). I will therefore dub it the christological inflection of the name of the Trinity.
- The pattern of naming that employs an open-ended plurality of triads has a special affinity with the third person of the Trinity, the person who brings the divine life to abundant fruition in eternity and time. I will therefore dub it the pneumatological inflection of the name of the Trinity.[5]

By the end of the chapter, I hope to have persuaded the reader that the most appropriate way to name the Trinity is by using an ensemble of three ways, or, to put it another way, that the name of the Trinity is best understood as one name in three inflections.

By the end of the chapter, I also hope to have demonstrated something else. Surprising though it may seem, the key to an adequate understanding of the Trinity is a proper estimate of the centrality and abiding significance of the Tetragrammaton for Christian faith. This will not mean, of course, that Christians should expect Jews to give their assent to this account of who God is. On the contrary, my proposal serves in some ways to intensify awareness of the humanly unbridgeable gulf that separates Christians and Jews. But it is my hope that this account of the name of the Trinity can provide a key for an understanding of the unity of the Bible that makes supersessionism unintelligible, and that makes it easier for Christians to resolve other problems of concern.[6]

The Theological Inflection of the Name of the Trinity

The name of the Holy Trinity is one name in three inflections. I begin with the theological inflection, the one that tends to "foreground" the first person of the Trinity, the person whose ineffable mystery and reliable identity are the Unoriginate Origin of the divine life and of all God's works in time. As we shall see, it belongs to the logic of this inflection to begin with the personal proper name of the One to whom Jesus prays and to proceed from there to tell us who Jesus and the Spirit eternally are: persons who likewise bear one and the same name, albeit in different ways.

At the heart of the theological inflection is a single word, the Holy Tetragrammaton, the final name that God gave to Moses at the burning bush. Without a doubt, the Tetragrammaton is a mysterious name, in part because it is surrounded by a host of unanswered—perhaps unanswerable—questions: What are the historical origins of the name? How was it originally pronounced? What etymological meaning does it have, if any? How is it related to the other names that God gave to Moses at the burning bush, "I am who I am" and "I am"? And so on. But these questions are not the genuine mystery of the name. At most, they point to the mystery, like the reports of the empty tomb point to the mystery of the resurrection. The genuine mystery of the Tetragrammaton is at once very simple and inexhaustibly deep: the Tetragrammaton is a personal proper name, like "Moses" or "Jesus" or "Mary Magdalene." As Michael Wyschogrod has written, *The God of Israel has a proper name.* There is no fact in Jewish theology more significant than this."[7] What Wyschogrod writes about Jewish theology is equally true of Christian theology.

A personal proper name is a humble thing. Unlike a metaphor, or a common noun, or a concept, a personal name need have little or no conventional meaning to do its work. The role of a personal name is not to define or describe but to identify—this one, and not another. If all you know about me is my name, you know very little indeed. That is the truth in the well-known expression

"What's in a name?" Yet the very humility of a personal name is the source of an unexpected strength. Because a personal name serves merely to signify "this one and not another," it can acquire a special kind of sense that arises from the history of its bearer. Over time, it can become saturated with a richness of connotation and resonance that exceeds any other form of human speech. The songwriter asks, "How do you find a word that means 'Maria'?" The point is you can't. For those who know and love her, the name "Maria" conveys a fullness and specificity of meaning that cannot be exhausted by any other word or description, no matter how apt. A personal proper name is the linguistic token that signifies the *who-ness* of a person in the indescribable fullness of his or her identity *and* mystery. That is why personal proper names have such astonishing power and dignity: *they are tokens of a person's unsubstitutable identity and uncircumscribable mystery at once.*

The Tetragrammaton is the personal proper name of the God of Israel, the Holy One to whom Jesus prays. That is its special mystery. Other names for God in the Scriptures of Israel are not personal proper names but common nouns, appellations, and epithets.[8] The Tetragrammaton alone is the linguistic token by which the God of Israel is distinguished from all other gods, indeed, from everything else altogether. In Catherine M. LaCugna's words, it is God's "self-given name."[9] Regardless of the name's etymology or historical origins, the sense of the Tetragrammaton in the Scriptures comes not from any conventional or generic meaning of the word but from the incomparable uniqueness of the God who bears it in eternity and in time. When the psalmist shouts, "Who is like the LORD our God?" (Ps 113:5), he is asking, in effect, "How do you find a word that means 'LORD'?" The impossibility of answering belongs to the sense of the Tetragrammaton. The mystery of this name corresponds not to reports of the empty tomb but to the resurrection itself, which of course the Gospels never narrate. It is therefore a fact of great significance that the Tetragrammaton appears almost seven thousand times in the Hebrew Bible, more than twice as often as all other designations for the Deity. It is no exaggeration to say that the hidden brilliance of this name illuminates the canon from beginning to end. The Dutch theologian and antifascist organizer Kornelis Heiko Miskotte was correct when he wrote, "In the building of scriptural vocabulary, [the Tetragrammaton] is the cornerstone and it possesses a miraculous supporting capacity. It binds even the most disparate parts together and gives these contradictions a gleam of certainty that has no human origin."[10]

According to Maimonides, the Tetragrammaton belongs on God's side of the distinction between eternity and time: it betokens God's eternal *who-ness* in a manner that is independent of God's relation to creation.[11] The statement "I am the LORD, that is my name" (Isa 42:8) is true in every possible world, as indeed it would be true were there no created world at all. At the same time, the Bible makes clear on page after page that a singular relationship exists between God's eternal identity and the chosen lineage descended from the patriarchs. This relation exists not by necessity but by grace. God's free election of Israel is the outworking of God's desire to be known by name. For the sake of this name, God fashions a people out of the barren womb of Sarah and out of the chaos of bondage, so that by works of steadfast love and faithfulness, God might be glorified by name not only in the heavens but also by men and women on the earth. The thickening cloud of connotation that the Tetragrammaton gradually reveals over time is thus finally eschatological in orientation. Under the pressure of God's great promise, "I will sanctify my great name" (Ezek 36:23), the Tetragrammaton points irresistibly forward to God's consummation of creation, when there will be an end to the state in which "all day long, [God's] name is despised" (Isa 52:5), and God's incomparable uniqueness will be fittingly honored by Israel, the nations, and all creation.

Now, for all of that, the Christian relationship to the Tetragrammaton has long been a checkered one, as we have already noted. On the one hand, since the Reformation era, at least, Western Christians generally recognized its importance for the Old

Testament and for Judaism, insofar as they have been aware of it at all. On the other hand, they have often never so much as suspected its continuing importance for the writers of the New Testament. In effect, they have perceived the Tetragrammaton as the quintessential mark of who God *was* but not of who God *is* and *will be.* The key reason for this is quite simple. As all students of the Greek New Testament know, the *written* Tetragrammaton is completely absent from its pages. This is true even when a New Testament author cites an Old Testament passage in which the Divine Name originally appeared. In its place, the reader typically encounters *kyrios*, or "Lord," without the definite article (we will have more to say about that shortly). When one compares the Name's absence in the New Testament to its ubiquity in the Old, it is easy to understand why Christian interpreters have often rejected the idea that the Tetragrammaton possesses any continued importance for Christian faith. In a tone of outraged common sense, the English poet John Milton demands,

> If that name [i.e., the Tetragrammaton] be so acceptable to God, that he has always chosen to consider it as sacred and peculiar to himself alone, why has he uniformly disused it in the New Testament, which contains the most important fulfilment of his prophecies; retaining only the name of Lord, which had always been common to him with angels and men? If, lastly, any name whatever can be so pleasing to God, why has he exhibited himself to us in the gospel *without any proper name at all?*[12]

What Milton overlooks is the possibility that the New Testament's "uniform disuse" of the written Tetragrammaton *is itself* a sign of its "sacred and peculiar" character. As Martin Luther was fond of emphasizing, the New Testament is the literary deposit of an oral communication. But the first propagators of that communication did not pronounce the Name any more than do pious Jews today. The most meticulous transcript of a modern synagogue service would not contain even a single instance of the written Tetragrammaton. What it would record instead would be *traces* of the Name—that is, pious circumlocutions used in its place, such as "Adonai" when Scripture was read aloud or *Hashem* ("the Name") in less formal contexts. And so it is with the documents of the New Testament. Consider this example from the Gospel of Mark, which provides a "transcript" of Jesus's trial before the high priest:

> Again the high priest asked him, "Are you the Messiah, the Son of the Blessed One?" Jesus said, "I am; and you will see the Son of Man seated at the right hand of the Power, and 'coming with the clouds of heaven.'" (Mark 14:61–62)

Here both the high priest and Jesus use surrogates in place of the Divine Name. "The Blessed" and "the Power" are not designations for the Deity that stand independently in their own right, such as "God" or "the Holy One of Israel," but stand-in names used in place of the Divine Name, which remains unspoken. Jesus and the high priest use different buffer names, but they have no difficulty understanding each other. Each knows that the other employs a buffer name precisely for the purpose of referring—silently but explicitly—to the One who bears the Divine Name. Divided by the question of Jesus's identity, Jesus and the high priest nevertheless share a common reverence for the Divine Name, a fact they signal by one and the same method: conspicuous avoidance of the Name itself.

Or consider the Lord's Prayer. We know, of course, that Jesus taught his followers to pray—first and before all else—for God's name to be hallowed (Matt 6:9). Still, we do not often fully consider what this implies about how Jesus *identifies* the One to whom he prays. Notice that Jesus formulates the first petition in the passive voice: "*Hallowed be* thy name." The same is true of the third petition, "Thy will *be done*." Even the second petition avoids directly referring to the agent of the desired action: "Thy kingdom come" (Matt 6:10 KJV; italics added). Jesus's use of the passive is to be understood in the context of Jesus's very Jewish reverence for God's name.[13] Jesus employs what biblical scholars have called the "divine passive" to call reverentially upon God in a manner that avoids mentioning God directly. Here the passive voice does not imply any ambiguity regarding *who* is being called upon to act. Quite the contrary. In the context of Second Temple piety for the name, Jesus's reverential use of the passive voice serves to identify—indirectly but unmistakably—the first petition's logical agent: the Deity whose name is the Tetragrammaton. The first petition is thus a kind of concentrated reiteration of the cumulative witness of the Old Testament. It is a plea that God will glorify the Divine Name with eschatological finality, in accord with the ancient promise, "Then you shall know that I am the LORD" (Exod 16:12; Jer 24:7; Ezek 36:11; etc.).[14]

We will explore Jesus's reverence for the Divine Name in greater detail later in this book. For now, the point to emphasize is this: The New Testament writers use these same forms of paraphrastic speech not only to identify the One to whom Jesus prays but also to identify Jesus and the Holy Spirit. They too are presented as bearers of the unspoken Name, each in a different way, by virtue of their relationship to the name's Unoriginate Bearer, the One to whom Jesus prays.

The New Testament provides many clues that identify the Spirit in terms of its origin from the God whose personal proper name is the Tetragrammaton. Some of these are relatively well known: the very phrase "Holy Spirit" derives from a reverential circumlocution, "the Spirit of holiness," an echo of which can still be heard in Paul's salutation in Romans: Jesus Christ, "designated Son of God in power according to the Spirit of holiness by his resurrection from the dead" (Rom 1:4 RSV). But other clues are often hidden from us by translation. Consider the story in which Peter remonstrates Sapphira and Ananias for deceitfully withholding money from the saints. Peter asks, "How is it that you have agreed together to tempt the *Spirit of Lord?*" (Acts 5:9; author's translation, italics added). Notice: "the Spirit of Lord," not "the

Spirit of the Lord." According to a rule of Greek grammar known as the Canon of Apollonius, two nouns in regimen should both have the definite article or both lack it. An exception occurs, however, when the second noun is a proper name, in which case the second article may be omitted.[15] Here the missing article is a signal that the Spirit proceeds from the God whose personal proper name is the Tetragrammaton. Not coincidentally, Sapphira falls down dead on the spot.

Most of all, the New Testament writers exploit the volatility of paraphrastic speech to make the astonishing claim that Jesus of Nazareth too is the bearer of the Divine Name, the Name that Jesus himself, according to the Fourth Gospel, characterizes in prayer as "your name *that you have given me*" (John 17:11, 12; italics added). The Synoptic Gospels make this claim in programmatic fashion by placing the words of John the Baptist near the beginning of their narratives: "Prepare the way of Lord, make his paths straight" (Matt 3:3; author's translation). Notice again: "the way of *Lord*," not "the way of *the Lord*." In this way, they make the point that the end-time glorification of the Divine Name for which Jesus prays is an event that coincides with the person and history of Jesus himself. At the close of the New Testament canon, the book of Revelation makes a similar point in an especially intricate way. In place of the customary Christian salutation "Grace and peace to you from God *our Father*," John the Seer writes, "Grace to you and peace from *He who was and who is and who is coming*" (Rev 1:4; author's translation, italics added). The italicized words appear in the nominative case in Greek, even though the salutation's syntax makes this a grammatical "error" of the most egregious kind. But there is no error: John purposefully uses a grammatical solecism to imply that the italicized phrase is a single indeclinable noun, like a Hebrew proper name.[16] The deviant grammar signals that the phrase stands in place of a proper name that does not appear on the surface of the text: the Tetragrammaton. (Once again, translators industriously mask the telltale oddity, in this case by pedantically correcting John's grammar; cf. "Grace to you and peace from *him* who is" [Rev

1:4 NRSV; italics added].) More strikingly still, John immediately breaks apart this conspicuous allusion to the Tetragrammaton and uses its elements to refer to *Jesus*. Just a few verses later,
Jesus declares, "I am the first and the last, and the living one" (Rev
1:17–18). John's point is that Jesus fulfills the promise implied in
the name of the Ancient of Days. Jesus is quite literally the one who
comes "in the name of Lord."[17]

In the next chapter, we will continue our exploration of this
pattern of naming, focusing on how it provides a way of thinking
about the eternal relation of the first and second persons of the
Trinity. But for now, this must suffice to introduce the theological
inflection of the name of the Trinity. This inflection begins with
the personal proper name of the One to whom Jesus prays, the Primordial Bearer of the Divine Name, and proceeds from there to tell
us who Jesus and the Spirit are: persons who likewise bear one and
the same name, each in a different way.

The Christological Inflection of the Name of the Trinity

A second pattern of naming the Trinity is distinguished from the
first by its characteristic vocabulary, which consists in a spare
selection of kinship terms—"Father" and "Son"—together with
an indispensable reference to the Holy Spirit. While the triad can
take many syntactic forms, it is given classic expression in the symmetrical phrase "the name of the Father and of the Son and of the
Holy Spirit," spoken by the risen Christ on an unnamed mountain
in Galilee (Matt 28:19). For this reason, and for others discussed
below, we will call this the christological inflection of the name
of the Trinity.

We already noted the disputed character of this triad at
the beginning of this chapter. What is sometimes overlooked is the
fact that partisans on both sides frequently share a good bit of common ground. Defenders of the baptismal triad generally concede to
feminists that as a matter of practice, the triad has in fact been misunderstood and abused in ways that are detrimental to women and
that Christians are obligated to reject and eliminate such misuses.

Feminists, in turn, generally concede to traditionalists that as a matter of principle, the baptismal triad can be interpreted in ways that are compatible with the affirmation of women's equality with men and that such uses should be fostered and encouraged. Underlying this tacit consensus (which is sometimes deeply masked) is the recognition by both parties of the possibilities and ambiguities that attend all analogical language for God, "the Father and the Son and the Holy Spirit" included.

But if so much common ground exists, is the conflict just a big misunderstanding? Not at all. Close inspection, however, suggests that the conflict is less about the proper use and misuse of the language of "the Father, the Son, and the Holy Spirit" per se than it is about *the status of this ternary within the total economy of Trinitarian names.* Traditionalists, for their part, typically argue that "Father and Son and Holy Spirit" is in fact *the* most appropriate way of naming the persons of the Trinity tout court. Progressives, in contrast, deny this while maintaining instead that "the Father, the Son, and the Holy Spirit" is one valid way of naming the persons of the Trinity among others. It is this *either-or* that gives the debate its extremely polarized character, which one theologian has called "as oppositional as any" today.[18] The genuine common ground that exists between the parties is masked, as the two contrary assessments of the place of male kinship terminology in Trinitarian discourse become the starting points for more global—and frequently antithetical—readings of Scripture, tradition, and the contemporary scene.

But is there no alternative to the polarizing *either-or*? The articulation of an alternative that recognized elements of truth in both positions would certainly not magically settle all the points of dispute between traditionalists and progressives regarding the status of male-gendered language for God. But it might make it possible to more easily claim the genuine common ground shared by all parties.[19]

My proposal is that the Spirit-enhanced kinship vocabulary of "Father" and "Son" is neither the most appropriate name of the

Trinity tout court nor simply one instance of many equally valid triads. Rather, it is the name of the Trinity in a distinctively *christological* modulation of voice. Its special charism is to illuminate the whole mystery of the Trinity in eternity and time in a way that "foregrounds" the second person and the glad tidings of mutual presence at the heart of the divine life. A key implication of this proposal is that it requires us to appreciate both how this inflection of the triune name is irreducibly distinct and how it is inseparably related to the other two equally important inflections. Let us examine both aspects of the christological inflection.

The christological inflection of the triune name is irreducibly distinct, incapable of equivalent substitution by any other form of expression. How so? Consider these points.

First, "the Father and the Son and the Holy Spirit" is irreducibly distinct by virtue of its canonical setting, where it appears in the context of the risen Lord's command to his disciples to baptize in this name (Matt 28:16–20). Furthermore, and as befits a formula intended for liturgical use, the phrase identifies the persons of the Trinity in a simple, fixed, and pronounceable form. In this respect, the christological inflection differs markedly from the theological inflection that we just considered. As we saw, the theological inflection is fecund, generative: the unspoken Tetragrammaton speaks through a variety of reverential circumlocutions. In contrast, the christological inflection gathers many forms of Jesus's speech—my Father, our Father, Son of Man, Son of God, Spirit of the Father, and so on—and stabilizes them in a single, coordinated phrase. These factors make the christological inflection uniquely suited to serve as a simple but tangible expression of the visible unity of the ecumenical church.[20]

Second, the christological inflection of the triune name is irreducibly distinct by virtue of its use of kinship vocabulary to designate the first two persons of the Trinity. Janet Soskice has suggested that the biblical writers employ gendered imagery for God not because they "were so very interested in sex, or even hierarchy and subordination, but because they were interested in kinship."[21] And indeed, the vocabulary of kinship possesses special characteristics that set it apart from other forms of speech. Unlike proper names and most common nouns, kinship terms are inherently reciprocal. It is possible but cumbersome to express the eternal relatedness of the first and second persons of the Trinity in the idiom of the theological inflection; one might speak, for example, of the "Giver and Receiver of the Divine Name." In contrast, naming the persons of the Trinity as "Father" and "Son" identifies them in a way that immediately signifies their relationship to each other. In this way, the christological inflection illuminates the mystery of the Trinity in a way that "foregrounds" the glad tidings of mutual loving presence at the heart of the divine life.

Third, this inflection is distinctive because it tends to illuminate the whole mystery of the Trinity from the perspective of the centrality of the second person. This is suggested by the simple fact that the words "the Son" appear in the middle of the baptismal triad, "the Father and the Son and the Holy Spirit," but it is also indicated by a closer analysis of the terms themselves. Consider that "the Father" identifies the first person in terms of a relation to the second but not the third person, since the first person is not the Father of the Spirit. (Indeed, "Spirit" is not a kinship term at all and thus interrupts and qualifies the vocabulary's kinship idiom.) And even when we consider the two kinship terms alone, "the Son" has a certain climactic significance, insofar as the kinship relation implied by the word "Father" is only actualized by the reality of the Son. Similarly, the Bible's divine kinship language does not serve to pick out who among the gods is the Father. That is a foregone conclusion. The Father is the One who bears the Divine Name: "You, O LORD, are our Father, our Redeemer from of old is your name" (Isa 63:16 ESV). Rather, its role is to pick out who among many possible contenders is the Son. That is where the emphasis falls in both Testaments: "*Israel* is my firstborn son" (Exod 4:22), "*This* is my Son" (Matt 3:17). In sum, if the theological inflection of the triune name orbits the first person of the Trinity as though around the source of the triune Life, the christological inflection orbits the second as though around its heart (cf. John 1:18).

Finally, the christological inflection is distinct because it identifies the second person in a way that underscores his unique role as the fulcrum of the "happy exchange" at the center of the economy of salvation. Only the second person of the Trinity assumes a human nature in order that a fallen humankind might be joined to the divine life. The vocabulary of kinship lends itself to expressing this truth in a powerful way. As Soskice has observed, kinship was of interest to the biblical writers because it "is all about birth, growth, and change."[22] To this I would add that it is all about birth *and* death, growth *and* loss, change for the better *and* change for the worse. In other words, kinship is a profoundly *ambiguous* phenomenon, the site of the most extreme possibilities both of violation, bitterness, and grief and of wholeness, satisfaction, and joy. This ambiguity, I suggest, is key for understanding what it means to affirm that Jesus of Nazareth is the eternal Son of God who becomes the child of Mary. The eternal Son assumes the vicissitudes of human kinship in order that Adam's fallen children might become the adopted sons and daughters of God. Here again, it is significant that it is the crucified and risen Christ who pronounces the phrase "the Father and the Son and the Holy Spirit." The name serves as the victorious pledge that the bond of divine kinship love is stronger than sin and death.

Yet now we must turn to the other side of the equation. Precisely because the christological pattern of naming the Trinity has a distinctive profile that foregrounds the second person, it cannot serve as the most appropriate way of naming the Trinity tout court. Treating it as such inevitably exposes its ambiguous vocabulary of kinship to exactly the sort of misunderstanding against which feminist theologians have warned. Rather, the integrity of the pattern depends on it being constantly chastened and clarified by countervailing pressure from other equally important inflections of the name of the Trinity. In the next section, we will examine the

Spirit-centered pattern of naming, which identifies the persons of the Trinity using a plenitude of common nouns drawn from the breadth of human experience, such as "God, Word, and Wisdom"; "Lover, Beloved, Love"; "Archetype, Image, Purifying Sun"; and so on. For now, I want to focus on the christological pattern's inseparable relation to the theological inflection, the pattern that orbits the personal proper name of the first person, the unspoken Tetragrammaton.

Let me begin with an obvious point. The kinship terms *father* and *son* can be predicated of many subjects. The christological inflection, however, particularizes the terms by using the definite article. It speaks not (as Christians often but misleadingly say) of "Father, Son, and Holy Spirit" but of "*the* Father and *the* Son and *the* Holy Spirit." The definite article particularizes the generic nouns by restricting their application from the many to the one. Nevertheless, the power of the definite article to particularize kinship terms is not absolute but dependent on a more complete framework of identification that terminates finally in a personal proper name. But what is the personal proper name that nominalizes "the Father and the Son and the Holy Spirit" and so rescues it from generic ambiguity? Is it, as Christians are no doubt inclined to suggest, the name "Jesus"? But the Marcionites also worshipped "the Father and the Son and the Holy Spirit" and backed up their worship with the name of Jesus! Nevertheless, the church deemed their worship heretical.[23] Moreover, the name "Jesus" belongs to the second person of the Trinity by virtue of God's works in time, while the name of the Father and the Son and the Holy Spirit belongs to the Trinity irrespective of those works. Hence, there must be some other personal proper name that backs up the christological inflection of the name of the Trinity. And that name can only be the Holy Tetragrammaton.

The New Testament witness confirms this conclusion on page after page. Time and again, we discover the vocabulary of "Father," "Son," and "Spirit" intertwined and interpreted by periphrastic language that silently signals the Tetragrammaton. "Our *Father* in heaven, hallowed be thy *name*" is not a redundant expression, as though "Father" were now the name of God tout court. Rather, the phrase points to distinct but mutually illuminating poles of Jesus's identification of God. Again, Paul affirms that Jesus is given "the name that is above every name" in order that he might receive creation's acclamation "*to the glory of God the Father*" (Phil 2:9, 11; italics added). The Fourth Gospel affirms that the Father's sending of the Son climaxes in the Son's revelation of the Father's *name* (John 17), which Raymond Brown identifies with the unspoken Tetragrammaton.[24] Finally, Dale C. Allison has suggested that even the baptismal formula of Matthew 28:19 alludes to the Tetragrammaton, inasmuch as "*the name of* the Father and of the Son and of the Holy Spirit" (italics added) is not an epexegetical reference to "the Father and the Son and the Holy Spirit" but rather a circumlocution for the unspoken Tetragrammaton—that is, the name that belongs to the Father and that the Father gives to the Son and whose praise is evoked by the Spirit of holiness.[25]

Conversely, when Christians read the Scriptures in a way that ignores this inseparable relatedness, they elevate the christological inflection in a perilously one-sided way. While Marcionism is the most extreme example of this tendency, a similar bent distorts much mid-twentieth-century theology. In 1933, the German theologian Gerhard Kittel wrote, "Everything that Christ taught, everything that makes the New Testament new, and better than the Old, everything that is distinctively Christian as opposed to merely Jewish, is summed up in the knowledge of the Fatherhood of God. 'Father' is the Christian name of God."[26] Kittel's claim was subsequently taken up in various ways by a generation of influential theologians, from Joachim Jeremias to Jürgen Moltmann. When, in the 1970s, feminist theologians and biblical scholars began to charge this line of interpretation with systematically distorting the biblical witness, they were surely right.

The Pneumatological Inflection of the Name of the Trinity

Our third and final pattern of naming the Trinity is also characterized by a distinctive vocabulary, which consists in a plenitude of common nouns drawn from human experience of the cosmos in all its depth, variety, and abundance across time and place. Like the previous patterns of naming, this pattern too is naturally associated with a scriptural site of sacred memory: the morning of Pentecost when God's Spirit was poured out on "all flesh," and people from every land heard "God's deeds of power" proclaimed "in [their] own languages" (Acts 2:11, 17). We will therefore call this pattern of naming the pneumatological inflection of the name of the Trinity.

Just as the Holy Spirit is sometimes reckoned the stepchild of the doctrine of the Trinity, so common nouns might seem at first glance to be little more than the leftovers of the theological lexicon. In reality, the biblical portrait of the Deity would immediately crumble to pieces if it consisted only in the Tetragrammaton and vocabulary of kinship. The latter is sparsely attested in the Old Testament and further whittled down in the New Testament to a single pair of terms which, however important, scarcely suffice to scaffold the biblical witness as a whole. The Tetragrammaton, for its part, is indeed the most frequently attested designation for the Deity in both Testaments (when one includes indirect allusions to it in the New), but it too suffers from a constitutional limitation: it is semantically opaque, a mute signifier whose hidden depths must be explicated by other means. This is what the plenitude of common nouns can do. This pattern of naming God repeats in its own luxuriously abundant idiom what the other inflections say in theirs and thereby brings them to fruition while at the same time rescuing them from obscurity and ambiguity. Beginning in the Old Testament with variants of the ordinary Semitic word for *god* (*el, elohim, eloha*, etc.), common nouns signify who God is by drawing from every sphere of human experience: "banner," "inheritance," "peace," "knowledge," "rock," "fortress," "deliverer," "king," "strength," "stronghold for the oppressed," "righteous," "refuge," "cup," "light," and so on.

This pattern of naming's delight in copious variation is especially evident in passages of Wisdom literature that proved influential for New Testament accounts of the preexistent Christ and for the later development of the doctrine of the Trinity. A set of remarkable texts portrays divine wisdom as a kind of heavenly consort who exists alongside God before the world's creation (Job 28; Prov 1, 8, 9; Bar 3:9–4:4; Sir 24; Wis 7:7–9:18). The precise nature of wisdom's origin from God is mysterious and obscure. It is described as a creating, setting up, coming forth, and so on—all in a single text (Prov 8:22–25 LXX). Adding to wisdom's mystery is her quicksilver persona. Though always concerned with the things that lead to life, she is sometimes concretely personal and other times immaterial and conceptual. Wisdom speaks out in the public streets like an Old Testament prophet, first threatening and cajoling, then comforting with food and wine (Prov 1:20–33, 9:1–6). In a more "demythologized" vein, she is described as "a breath of the power of God," "a pure emanation of the glory of the Almighty," "a reflection of eternal light," and "an image of his goodness" (Wis 7:22, 25–26) who confers "immortality," "joy," and "gladness" (Wis 8:16–17).

The New Testament writers, in turn, echo wisdom tradition's rich vocabulary of common nouns in their descriptions of the preexistent Christ while generally eschewing the kinship vocabulary of "Father" and "Son" for this purpose (as does wisdom tradition itself). They are especially drawn to wisdom speculation in its "demythologized" form. The preexistent Christ is said to be "the image of the invisible God" (Col 1:15), "the reflection of God's glory," "the exact imprint of God's very being" (Heb 1:3), "in the form of God" (Phil 2:5), and, of course, "the Word" (John 1:1, 18) who "sustains all things" (Heb 1:3) and brings "peace" (Col 1:20), "life," and "light" (John 1:4). While New Testament accounts of the Holy Spirit are less directly dependent on wisdom tradition, they too show considerable linguistic variation, as in "Spirit of truth"

(John 14:17), "Spirit of life" (Rom 8:2), "Spirit of the living God" (2 Cor 3:3), "Spirit of grace" (Heb 10:29), "spirit of glory" (1 Pet 4:14), and so on.

Considering this broad stream of testimony, it is not surprising that the first Christian theologians to reflect extensively on God's pretemporal relation to Christ and the Spirit, the second-century apologists, did so using the vocabulary of common nouns drawn from wisdom tradition. As Maurice Wiles has pointed out, for the apologists, "the ideas of God and his Word or God and his Wisdom" were much more important than "the idea of God the Father and his Son."[27] Tatian, for example, never uses the term "Son" in his *Address to the Greeks*, and Theophilus does so only rarely in *Apology to Autolycus*. Instead, both theologians prefer to speak of Christ as the first-begotten word or wisdom of God. The apologists' attraction to this vocabulary is so pronounced that it accounts for another name by which they are commonly known: Logos-theologians. The Logos-theologians' choice of conceptuality is often chalked up to the fact that they were seeking to make Christian faith intelligible and attractive to their Hellenistic contemporaries, and no doubt this is true. The concept of a divine Logos was well-established in the Hellenistic world, whereas the New Testament's language of "Father" and "Son" was easily misunderstood in a pagan context replete with sometimes lurid stories of divine kinship. Still, on this score at least, we cannot fairly accuse the apologists of abandoning Scripture for Hellenistic fashion, for they were in fact echoing *the Bible's own most common way* of naming God and God's own pretemporal counterpart.

In time, the Nicene Creed would canonize this pattern of naming the persons of the Trinity by identifying God as "Light," Christ as "Light from Light," and the Spirit as "the Giver of life." Yet the pattern itself flourished long before the council met and has continued to do so since. Here are a few instances chosen more or less at random: "God, Inward Meditation, Wisdom" (Theophilus); "Annointer, Annointed, Unction" (Irenaeus); "that which is without beginning, that which is the beginning, and that which is with the beginning," "Unoriginate, Unoriginately Begotten, Unbegottenly Proceeding," "out of Light, Light, in Light," "Producer, Offspring, Product," "Unbegotten, Begotten, One which Proceeds" (Gregory of Nazianzus); "Fountain, River, Drink," "Light, Radiance, Enlightenment" (Athanasius); "Mother of the Bridegroom, Sophia, Mother Dove," "the First, the One which Depends on the First, and that One which is through that which depends on the First," "that from which the Word and Spirit is, Word, Spirit" (Gregory of Nyssa); "Beautiful Source, Image of the Invisible God, Spirit of Knowledge" (Basil of Caesarea); "Eternity, Truth, Love," "Source, Intellect, Emanation," "Origo, Informatio, Beatitudo," "Eternity, Eternal Truth, Eternal and True Love" (Augustine); "Eternal Light, Splendor of Eternal Light, Burning Fire" (Ambrose); "Infinity in the Eternal, Beauty in the Image, Value in the Gift" (Hilary of Poitiers); "Fire, Light, Warmth" (Ephrem the Syrian); "Unity, Truth, Loving-kindness"; "Eternity, Appearance, Event"; "Principle, Exposition, Consummation"; "All-power, All-knowledge, Goodwill" (Bonaventure); "eternal sovereign truth, eternal sovereign wisdom, eternal sovereign love," "Might, Wisdom, Love," "Joy, Bliss, Delight," "Maker, Keeper, Lover," "Being, Increase, Fulfillment," "Nature, Mercy, Grace," "Fatherhood, Motherhood, Lordship" (Julian of Norwich); "a Brightness, a Flashing Forth, a Fire" (Hildegard of Bingen); "Deep of the Omnipotence, Deep of Uncreated Wisdom, Breath-taking Goodness" (Gertrude of Helfta); "the One who Kisses, the One who is Kissed, the Kiss" (Bernard of Clairvaux); "our Table, our Food, our Server," "Light, Wisdom, and Strength" (Catherine of Siena); "Unground, Ground, and Intuition" (Jacob Boehme); "Origin, Wisdom, Power" (Calvin); "Deus intelligens, Deus intellectus, Deus dilectus" (William Ames); "God, Idea, Delight and Energy" (Jonathan Edwards); "light divine, radiance, all-quickening breath" (Charles Wesley); "God, Expositor, Spirit," "Author, Actor, Director," "the One, the Other, and the Unifying" (von Balthasar); "Utterer, Utteréd, Uttering" (Gerard Manley Hopkins); "Source, Dramatic Coherence, Freedom," "Hope, Fulfillment, and Faithfulness" (Robert Jenson); "the One Before Us, the One with Us, the

One Ahead of Us" (Segundo); "Giver, Given, Giving," "Speaker, Spoken, Hearing," "Lover, Loved, and Loving," "Self-Giver, Self-Given, Self-Giving" (Paul Hinlicky); "Mother Sophia, Jesus Sophia, Spirit Sophia," "Unoriginate Love, Love from Love, Mutual Love" (Elizabeth A. Johnson); "Source, Issue, Response" (Rowan Williams); "Beginning, Middle, End," "Holiness, Mercy, Loving-Kindness," "the One who rules and commands in majesty, the One who obeys in humility, the One who maintains his fellowship with himself as the One and the Other" (Karl Barth); "Fountain, Offspring, and Wellspring," "Womb of Life and Source of Being, Life of Life and Death of Death, Brooding Spirit" (Ruth Duck); "playwright, actor, and producer" (Wesley Vander Lugt); "Breather, Breathing, Breath" (Sylvia Dunstan); "Namer, Named, Name Sharing" (Stanley Grenz); "of whom, through whom, in whom" (Gail Ramshaw).[28]

Yet granted that this pattern of naming the Trinity has an impeccable pedigree and is amply attested, why suggest that it has any special connection with the Holy Spirit? In fact, the connection between the Holy Spirit and common nouns is profound. The Holy Spirit is sometimes called the nameless person of the Trinity, but what this really means is that it is characteristic of the Holy Spirit to be named personally by means of nouns that are common to the other persons of the Trinity. Each person of the Trinity is "Holy," each person is "Spirit." Still, as Augustine observed, it is especially characteristic of the third person to take what is held in common and to "personalize" it, thereby giving it a hypostatic reality of its own that brings superabundant fullness and fruition to the life of the Trinity. In this case, what is "common" to the first two patterns of naming is their capacity to identify all three persons of the Trinity, which the Holy Spirit "personalizes" in its own native idiom, the plenitude of common nouns.

Furthermore, this pattern of naming is justly appropriated to the Holy Spirit because just as the Spirit proceeds from the first person and through the second (I hold the Eastern view of the eternal procession of the Spirit), so this pattern of naming does not bypass or ignore the two patterns that we have already discussed but pours forth from and through them as their indispensable expositor, purifier, and interpreter. Just as the Trinity is not "complete" without the procession of the Spirit, so the first pattern of naming is mute and the second fatally exposed to misunderstanding and abuse apart from the third.

Finally, this pattern of naming has a special affinity with the Holy Spirit because it belongs to it to ensure that "God's deeds of power" are heard in tongues that are appropriate to every time and place. Unlike the other patterns, the pneumatological pattern has no permanently fixed vocabulary of its own. Rather, it unfolds the glory of the triune Life in ever-new forms, making use of existing forms of speech and creating new possibilities of speech in the discourse of all peoples, generations, and cultures.

"These Three Are One"

The name of the Trinity is one name in three inflections, a polyphonic unity of three patterns of naming that are irreducibly distinct in themselves and inseparably related to one another.

The theological inflection identifies all three persons of the Holy Trinity in terms of the unspoken Tetragrammaton, the proper name that signifies the ineffable mystery and identity of the One to whom Jesus prays, the name that the Holy One gives to the person of Jesus, that is glorified by the Spirit of holiness, and by virtue of which the Holy Trinity is itself perfectly and simply one (cf. Deut 6:4). When we call upon the name of the Trinity in the idiom of the unspoken Name, we draw closer to the voice that spoke from the burning bush, that accompanies the people Israel through the ages, and that will declare at the dawn of the new age, "Behold, I make all things new" (Rev 21:5 RSV).

The christological inflection identifies all three persons of the Trinity in the light of Jesus the Son, who became a member of the broken human family in order that it might be adopted into his. When we call upon the name of the Trinity in the idiom of the baptismal name, we are drawn closer to the mystery of mutual love at the heart of the divine life and deeper into our baptismal vocation as adopted sons and daughters of God the Father and brothers and sisters of Jesus Christ.

The pneumatological inflection identifies all three persons of the Trinity in the light of the endless artistry of the Holy Spirit, the great Expositor of the divine life in eternity and in time. When we call upon the name of the Trinity in the idiom of the pneumatological inflection, we are drawn more deeply into the evangelical possibilities of our time and place and bidden so to use them that all may testify that "in our own languages we hear them speaking about God's deeds of power" (Acts 2:11).

✿ 3 ✿

ELECTION

THE PROPER NAME OF THE WORD WHO BECAME FLESH: THE TRINITY AND ELECTION DEBATE

Suppose that instead of giving us just one most appropriate way to name the persons of the Trinity, the Bible gave us three. Each pattern of naming told the truth, the whole truth, and nothing but the truth, but each did so with a vocabulary that had a special affinity with one person of the Trinity in particular. Suppose, furthermore, that Christians lost track of one of these three ways of naming—say, the one with an affinity for the first person, the One to whom Jesus prayed—because of the church's ancient estrangement from the Jewish people. What difference would this make for Christian theology more generally?

A possible answer might be "not much." After all, the church would still have two other ways of naming the Trinity, and these together could ensure the basic soundness of Christian worship, practice, and reflection. On the other hand, perhaps the consequences would be more severe, as the consequences of estrangement often are. Perhaps the absence of the missing pattern of naming would create problems that couldn't be solved by the remaining patterns alone, beginning with the lack of a proper account of the church's relationship to the Jewish people. And perhaps, from this initial problem, others would eventually arise to trouble the church's faith and practice.

In fact, I think this latter scenario is the one that obtains in reality. Holy Writ gifts the church with three equally basic ways of naming the Trinity, but Christians have been mostly color-blind to one of them, with consequences that reach through the whole tapestry of Christian theology. By retrieving the neglected pattern, however, Christians can begin to restore the tapestry to a deeper and more natural symmetry and perhaps even begin to repair the estrangement that caused the symmetry to be lost in the first place.

In this chapter, I want to explore this thesis with reference to a doctrine that serves as a hinge between the doctrine of the Trinity and the doctrines of creation, redemption, and consummation. The hinge is the doctrine of predestination, also known as the doctrine of God's eternal decree. Traditionally, the doctrine was most prominent among Reformed Christians, but it has come to the attention of Christians more generally thanks to the Reformed theologian Karl Barth, whose extraordinary reconceptualization of the doctrine of predestination is widely regarded as his single most important contribution to Christian theology.

In particular, the chapter will focus on a technical question of academic theology that has arisen in the wake of Barth's account of the eternal decree. The question goes this way: "Is the Trinity complete in itself from all eternity and apart from God's determination to become incarnate in Jesus Christ, or is it constituted by the eternal decision of election?"[1] The question arises in two contexts. First, what did Karl Barth think, and second, what should Christians think, regardless of what Barth thought?

Formidable theologians have lined up on either side of both questions. According to the leading Barth scholar Bruce McCormack, God's election to be God-for-us in the man Jesus is constitutive of the one God's threefold personhood as the Father, the Son, and the Holy Spirit.[2] McCormack maintains that this was Barth's mature view and the view best suited to orthodoxy in the modern era. According to the leading Barth scholar George Hunsinger, on the other hand, God's antecedent identity as the Father, Son, and Spirit logically grounds the divine decree to be God-for-us in the man Jesus.[3] Hunsinger maintains that Barth held this position throughout his life and that it is the strongest position overall.

My own view of the matter is quickly stated. I think that the Trinity is eternally complete apart from God's eternal decree of grace in Jesus Christ. I think that this was Barth's own consistent view and that it is the soundest position overall. At the same time, I think that Bruce McCormack and those who share his position have correctly identified a crucially important aspect of Barth's thought. In his doctrine of election, Karl Barth was trying to wring a dangerous ambiguity out of how Christians think about the eternal identity of the God who elects. McCormack thinks this Barthian impulse is worth championing, and I agree. However, I believe there is a better way of achieving what McCormack is after, one that avoids some of the ambiguities of Barth's own position. Rather than make the Trinity dependent on the covenant of grace, as McCormack proposes, we should instead address the problem by reclaiming the pattern of naming the persons of the Trinity that Christians have traditionally neglected, the one whose special charism lies in expressing the unsubstitutable uniqueness of the Trinity both in eternity and in time.

Let us begin by examining the neglected pattern of naming in greater detail.

Three Patterns of Naming the Persons of the Trinity

Sacred Scripture gives us three equally important ways of naming the persons of the Holy Trinity. Each pattern of naming is rooted in the Old Testament, flowers in the New, and is centered on the Gospels' portraits of Jesus's own characteristic ways of speaking about himself, the Spirit, and the One to whom he prays.

One way Jesus speaks about these three is by means of kinship terms. He addresses the One to whom he prays as "Father" (cf. Matt 11:25, Luke 23:46), which in turn highlights a corresponding way of identifying Jesus himself, as "Son" (Luke 9:35). The terms suggest a related way of identifying the Spirit—as the Spirit of the kinship relation that exists between this Father and this Son.

Another way Jesus typically speaks of God, himself, and the Spirit is by means of a variety of common nouns drawn from everyday life. We see this pattern of speech exemplified by Jesus's parables of the kingdom of God and by the wisdom hymns of the

Epistles and the Gospel of John, in which Jesus (to speak only of him) is called "Word" (John 1:1), "Image" (2 Cor 4:4), "Reflection" (Heb 1:3), "Exact Imprint" (Heb 1:3), and so on. Saints and theologians have developed this pattern of naming the Trinity by a countless host of ternaries, such as "God, Word, and Wisdom"; "Lover, Beloved, Love"; "Rose, Blossom, Fragrance"; and so on.

The third and final way Jesus speaks about God is less familiar to Christians than the previous two, chiefly because of this curiosity: it revolves around a word that Jesus scrupulously avoids saying. That word, of course, is the Tetragrammaton. The Tetragrammaton is neither a kinship term like *Father* nor a common noun like *God* or *King*. It is a personal proper name, composed of the four Hebrew letters *yod*, *heh*, *vav*, and *heh*. For as long as we know, Jews have regarded this as the most sacred name of God, by a wide stretch. Curiously enough, this is not because the word has a particularly remarkable meaning; indeed, it is not certain that it has any meaning at all. The famous "I am who I am" of Exodus 3:14 is an elucidating pun that anticipates the Tetragrammaton, not the Tetragrammaton itself.[4] Rather, the Tetragrammaton's significance resides in the fact that it is the personal proper name of *God*. Unlike appellatives and titles such as *God*, *King*, and *Father*, which apply to many besides the one true God, the Tetragrammaton clings to God alone and so is the mark of God's unsubstitutable identity par excellence.

Significantly, the Bible knows of no event in eternity or time when the Deity began to bear the name *yod heh vav heh*. YHWH became the Creator by creating. YHWH became "the God of Israel" by a gracious act of election. But the Bible never suggests that YHWH *became* YHWH at all. Instead, YHWH simply *is* the One who bears this name: "I am the Lord, that is my name; my glory I give to no other" (Isa 42:8). Within the Bible's frame of reference, the primordiality of the Tetragrammaton is absolute. Of course, this is not evident from the conventional surrogate *Lord*, which much rather implies a relationship of authority into which God enters contingently. But then *Lord* is a *surrogate* for the Divine Name, not the name itself. Here the elucidating pun of Exodus 3:14 has its relevance: "I am who I am." The purpose of wordplay is to anticipate and frame our understanding of the name that immediately follows, the Tetragrammaton (Exod 3:15).

While the Divine Name appears almost seven thousand times in the Old Testament, it never appears in the New Testament because its writers signify it obliquely, by means of a variety of surrogates, circumlocutions, and silent allusions. There is nothing surprising about this; the practice was typical of the Second Temple era. What is surprising, to say the least, is that the New Testament writers use such oblique references to indicate that the Tetragrammaton is borne not only by the One to whom Jesus prays but also by *Jesus himself.* How can this possibly be?

Most New Testament passages make no apparent effort to answer this question and merely affirm that it is so. Among these is 1 Corinthians 8:6, where Paul takes the Shema, Israel's ancient confession of faith in YHWH's oneness ("Hear O Israel, the Lord our God, the Lord is one" [Deut 6:4 TLV]), and reformulates it to *include* Jesus Christ: "For us there is one God . . . and one Lord, Jesus Christ." The result is a Christianized version of the Shema in which Jesus appears *inside* Israel's confession of faith in the oneness of the God who bears the Tetragrammaton. That it is appropriate to think of Jesus in this way, however, is something that Paul assumes rather than explains.

In contrast, at least two New Testament passages seem to have been designed to shed light on how it is possible for the Tetragrammaton to belong both to Jesus and to the God to whom he prays. The passages provide what is at heart a simple explanation: the One to whom Jesus prays has *given* it to Jesus, with the result that Jesus bears the Tetragrammaton as his own name. One text in which we encounter this idea is Philippians 2:5–11, one of the oldest writings in the New Testament:

> *Let the same mind be in you that was in Christ Jesus,*
> *who, though he was in the form of God,*

did not regard equality with God
as something to be exploited,
   but emptied himself,
taking the form of a slave,
being born in human likeness.
   And being found in human form,
he humbled himself
and became obedient to the point of death—
even death on a cross.

   Therefore God also highly exalted him
and gave him the name
that is above every name,
   so that at the name of Jesus
every knee should bend,
in heaven and on earth and under the earth,
   and every tongue should confess
that Jesus Christ is Lord,
to the glory of God the Father. (Phil 2:5–11)

Over the centuries, Christians have interpreted the name that God gave to Jesus—"the name that is above every name" (Phil 2:9)—in different ways. Some have held that the name is actually God's namelessness; others, that it is the august title *Lord*; and others, that it is the name "Jesus." When one considers the fact that Paul was a Jew writing in the context of Second Temple Judaism, however, a far more likely possibility presents itself. "The name that is above every name" refers quite obviously to the Tetragrammaton, the name that first-century Jews regarded as self-evidently God's most important name and that, therefore, they always referred to *obliquely*, by means of phrases such as "the name that is above every name." If this is correct, then Paul employs the Tetragrammaton to identify what Christians will later call the three persons of the Trinity. The One who raised Jesus from the dead (the first person) bears the Divine Name primordially and is in a position to give it to Jesus; Jesus (the second person) bears it receptively because he received it from the One who raised him from the dead; and the Spirit (the third person) proceeds from the first person and alerts creation to the fact that Jesus bears the Divine Name to the glory of the One who gave it to him. True, Paul does not explicitly mention the "Spirit of holiness" (Rom 1:4 RSV) in Philippians 2, but he implies its presence and activity when he writes that the whole cosmos will confess Jesus to be "Lord" (another conventional surrogate for the Tetragrammaton), a cry that Paul says elsewhere is possible only by the inspiration of the Holy Spirit (1 Cor 12:3).

Impressive though it is, the proto-Trinitarian "grammar" of Philippians 2:5–11 exhibits a troublesome feature when judged from the perspective of the church's mature doctrine of the Trinity. It suggests that Jesus *became* the bearer of the Divine Name at a certain point in time, unlike the person who gave him the name, who of course has borne it forever. Furthermore, it implies that the One who has borne the name forever *became* the *giver* of the name at the same point in time. Taken at face value, this points in the direction of adoptionism rather than Nicene orthodoxy, which affirms that the first person of the Trinity eternally communicates the divine essence to the second person and thereby generates the second's unique hypostatic identity. While we need not judge that Philippians 2 *requires* an adoptionist interpretation, we must certainly admit that it does not invite us to conceive of the giving and receiving of the Divine Name as an *eternal* event that mirrors the Father's eternal generation of the Son.

The Gospel of John presents things differently. Unlike the Christ hymn of Philippians, the Fourth Evangelist relates a giving and receiving of the Divine Name that is *manifested* in time but whose foundation is eternal.

John 17 records Jesus's prayer in the garden of Gethsemane on the eve of his crucifixion. At the beginning and end of the prayer, Jesus speaks of himself as having revealed the Divine Name, which he refers to as "*your* name"—that is, the name of the One to whom he prays (John 17:6, 26; italics added). In the middle of the prayer, however, Jesus refers to the Divine Name in a way that indicates that it is his name too. Twice in close proximity, as though to lend the phrase special emphasis, he calls it "your name *that you have given me*" (John 17:11, 12; italics added), using the perfect tense to indicate a completed action whose consequences continue into the present. I judge "your name that you have given me" to be among the most profoundly illuminating phrases in the Fourth Gospel and, indeed, in the entire New Testament. The phrase is designed to cast an explanatory light on the most wondrous truth that the New Testament reports. Jesus comes among human beings as the bearer of the Tetragrammaton because the One to whom it originally belongs has given it to Jesus to bear as his own.[5]

But granted that John 17 reports that God (the first person) has a name that he has given to Jesus, why should we think that it is the Tetragrammaton? And even if it is, why should we think that God's giving of this name is an eternal "event"? The Fourth Gospel is a virtual treasure chest of clues that indicate both things with the subtlety of a lightning bolt.[6] Recall that the Fourth Gospel portrays Jesus repeatedly declaring the words "I am" (*eigo eimi*). Seven times, Jesus declares, "I am," followed by some predicate of salvation, such as "the bread of life" (John 6:35), "the light of the world" (8:12), and so on. But seven times, Jesus simply says, "I am," *without any predicate at all*. The words just hang there, as odd sounding in Greek as they are in English. (The deliberate oddness is often blunted in translation by supplying the gratuitous predicate "he"—i.e., "I am he"; cf. John 8:24 NRSV.) This feature of the Fourth Gospel must be understood in light of Old Testament passages that link the phrase "I am" with the Tetragrammaton.[7] Far from being limited to Exodus 3:14–15, such passages are quite common in the LXX thanks to God's ubiquitous declaration "I am Lord!" (*ego eimi kyrios*). These passages employ the surrogate *kyrios* without an article to underscore its function as a stand-in for God's proper name. The saying "I am Lord" is especially characteristic of Isaiah 40–55, where it underscores the Lord's incomparable uniqueness and proven character as the Creator, Redeemer, and Consummator of all things. Significantly, Isaiah several times employs just the phrase "I am," all by itself, as an abbreviated, emphatic form of the longer self-declaration "I am Lord" (41:4; 46:4; etc.). The abbreviated form is materially identical to the longer one: "I am" = "I am Lord." On three occasions, the LXX goes so far as to render God's self-declaration with the extraordinary phrase "I am I am" (LXX: *ego eimi ego eimi*). So, for example, Isaiah 43:25 (LXX) reads,

> *I am I am [Gk: ego eimi ego eimi]*
> *who blots out your transgressions for my own sake,*
> *and I will not remember your sins.*

In this passage and similar ones, Second Isaiah creates a synonymy between "I am" and the Tetragrammaton, which is understood even when it is not explicitly mentioned. While the author of Second Isaiah wrote before the practice of avoiding God's name became customary, the synonymy he created has obvious relevance for the Gospel of John, which was written at a time when the custom was universally normative among Jews. As Charles Gieschen has written, "Although the EIGO EIMI formula in John should not be understood as the Divine Name that Jesus is said to have been given (17:6), nevertheless these absolute sayings are very closely related to it and function as a way of indicating that Jesus is the possessor of the Divine Name."[8] Distinct from God's personal name yet synonymous with it, the phrase "I am" permits Jesus to evoke God's name while leaving the name itself unspoken.

It would be rewarding to dwell on the "I am" statements in detail, but space requires that we limit ourselves to two passages. The first is this: "Amen I tell you, before Abraham was, I am" (John 8:58 TLV).

Clearly, the passage indicates that Jesus is "I am" before the foundation of the world. But if "I am" alludes to the Tetragrammaton, as it surely does, then Jesus must have been given this name before the foundation of the world. In short, the Fourth Gospel portrays the giving and receiving of the Divine Name as an eternal event. Jesus reveals himself to be the bearer of the Divine Name in time, but he was given it in eternity. The giving and receiving of the Divine Name are exactly isomorphic with what later Trinitarian tradition will understand as the Father's eternal generation of the Son and the Word's eternal procession from God. The three patterns of naming say the same thing using different vocabularies. At the same time, each vocabulary has a special charism of its own. In my judgment, the special charism of the vocabulary of the Divine Name is that it emphasizes the transcendent uniqueness of the persons of the Trinity. What makes the persons of the Trinity one and equally worthy of worship is the one name they share, the sacred Tetragrammaton (cf. the Shema). What distinguishes them is the different ways they share it: one as its primordial giver, one as its primordial receiver, one as the Spirit of its primordial glorification.

The other passage I want to examine briefly is this: "Then Jesus, knowing all that was to happen to him, came forward and asked them, 'Whom are you looking for?' They answered, 'Jesus of Nazareth.' Jesus replied, 'I am.' Judas, who betrayed him, was standing with them. When Jesus said to them, 'I am,' they stepped back and fell to the ground. Again he asked them, 'Whom are you looking for?' And they said, 'Jesus of Nazareth.' Jesus answered, 'I told you that I am'" (John 18:4–8).[9]

What is extraordinarily fascinating here is the interplay between the two names "I am" and "Jesus." The soldiers identify the one they are looking for by the mortal name "Jesus," which means "YHWH is Salvation." But they do not really know who the bearer of this mortal name is until he says, "I am," a revelation that forces them to the ground. (This is another allusion to Second Isaiah: "Turn to me and be saved. . . . To me every knee shall bow" [Isa 45:22–24 LXX].) "Jesus" and "I am" refer to the same person, but they are not exactly synonymous, any more than are "Jesus" and "Word" (John 1:1) or "son of Mary" and "Son of God." The person who declares "I am" is the eternal receiver of the Tetragrammaton in every possible world. He is *Ye-shua*, "YHWH is Salvation," in every world into which he is sent to save.

The Trinity and Election Debate

Back to the contemporary debate about Trinity and election. Many talented theologians have spilled a lot of ink on the topic, and to suggest at this late date that biblical exegesis might nudge things forward is to risk being lambasted by all sides. Still, that is what I want to propose. First, the debate itself.

Theologians today are discussing the nexus of Trinity and election because of Karl Barth. Specifically, they are doing so because of Barth's decision to subject the inherited doctrine of double predestination to a massive reworking in part 2 of *Church Dogmatics*, volume 2.[10] Karl Barth undertook this revision because of a single overriding concern: the inherited doctrine left the identity of the Trinity as the subject of election shrouded in obscurity and ambiguity. The doctrine of election could not be good news because the God at its foundation was not manifestly the God of the gospel, the God of Jesus Christ. Of course, Barth did not accuse the tradition of having a completely naked and *un*determined concept of the electing God. It certainly did not. The tradition affirmed with all clarity that the eternal subject of election is the Holy Trinity, and it filled out its account of the Trinity with a host of biblically attested names, such as Father, Son, Spirit, God, Word, and Image, not to mention a bristling army of elucidating concepts such as *logos asarkos, ensarkos, incarnandus,* and so on. Still, in Barth's view, the resulting portrait of the eternal subject of election remained dangerously ambiguous and *under*determined.

Dangerously underdetermined from what point of view? Barth is crystal clear: underdetermined from the point of view of "the name of Jesus Christ."[11] This point is worth emphasizing. To a degree that can scarcely be overstated, Barth developed his doctrine of election as a sustained meditation on a single biblically attested *proper name.* Barth had adopted a similar strategy once before in *Church Dogmatics,* in his influential account of the doctrine of the Trinity in volume 1. In that case, Barth argued that the doctrine of the Trinity was nothing more or less than an "explanatory confirmation" of "the revealed name *Yahweh-Kyrios*."[12] The name is clearly intended to signal the bicanonical significance of the Tetragrammaton, and I will have more to say about that claim later. For now, the point to note is that Barth makes no mention of *Yahweh-Kyrios* in his doctrine of election, as though the name itself had disappeared. Instead, he argues relentlessly that the doctrine of election is to be unfolded as a meditation on the name "Jesus Christ." It is the light of this name, Barth declares, that will banish the obscurity that has clouded the identity of the electing God and will disclose the God of love and freedom revealed in the gospel.

Seen against this backdrop, there is a certain inevitability to Barth's thesis that "Jesus Christ is the electing God and the elected human."[13] The thesis makes the name "Jesus Christ" decisive for the doctrine of election by using it to identify both the subject and the object of the act of election. In this way, Barth hoped, he would banish all obscurity from our conception of the eternal identity of the electing God.

Unfortunately, there is something rather obscure about Barth's thesis itself, and especially about its first half. The claim that Jesus Christ is the electing God turns the doctrine of election into a kind of Möbius strip, perpetually turning back on itself in a bewildering way. A temporally qualified outcome appears to be invoked as its own eternal starting point. I remember becoming almost dizzy when I first pondered the thesis as a graduate student. A friend and I chewed over it one sunny afternoon for what seemed like hours. I do not recall that we ended up more enlightened than when we began.

One of the merits of the vigorous debate conducted by Bruce McCormack, George Hunsinger, and others is to have clarified our understanding of the basic issues at stake. Here we can take our starting point from Bruce McCormack's formulation of Barth's insight: "The second person of the Trinity has a name, and his name is Jesus Christ."[14] But the thorny question is this: How does the second person of the Trinity become the bearer of this name? Does it belong to him by virtue of the same ontological necessity that makes the second person of the Trinity the second person? Or does it belong to him by virtue of a divine decision that is logically "downstream" of that necessity, by virtue of which the second person *becomes* Jesus Christ (cf. John 1:14) for us and for our salvation? Or, to put the matter as simply as possible, might the second person of the Trinity have been the second person without being Jesus Christ? And if so, who then would he have been?

Now, here is my contention. Our effort to give an adequate answer to these questions is hobbled—not crippled but hobbled—precisely insofar as we have become color-blind to the scriptural pattern of naming the Trinity that orbits the unspoken Tetragrammaton.

Suppose we say, with Paul Molnar and George Hunsinger, that the second person of the Trinity could have been the second person without bearing the name "Jesus Christ." This contention has the important and to my mind decisive advantage that it preserves the freedom and gratuity of the covenant of grace. Nevertheless, the position has an Achilles' heel. The difficulty appears when we try to speak in a biblically convincing manner about who the second person is prior to and apart from the proper name "Jesus." It is not that we lack a biblical vocabulary to answer this question. The problem, rather, is with limitations inherent in the vocabulary itself. We may say that the second person is the eternal Son, Word, Image, and so on, and we may buttress this by speaking of the other persons of the Trinity as Father, Spirit, Love, Gift, and so on. But the difficulty is that kinship terms and common nouns are applicable by nature to endlessly many subjects in heaven and on earth. History teems with fathers, sons, and spirits who have been worshipped and adored. So long as we specify the Trinity's eternal identity by means of such generic terms *alone*, we are left with a version of the problem that troubled Karl Barth in the first place. We are left with a picture of the eternal subject of election that is not false but *ambiguous and underdetermined.*

But suppose we say, with Bruce McCormack, that it is constitutive of the second person's eternal hypostatic identity to bear the name "Jesus," that the second person bears this name simply by virtue of being the second person at all. This contention has the advantage of addressing at full throttle the problem of an under-determined picture of the eternal Trinity. But it is a correction that comes at an exorbitant price. As many have pointed out, it makes the eternal Trinity wholly contingent on the decision to be for us and for our salvation and so impoverishes our ability to express the freedom and gratuity with which the Trinity freely chooses to create, redeem, and consummate. That is a remedy that is worse than the disease it is meant to cure.

In my opinion, McCormack is right to share Barth's sus-picions of underdetermined accounts of God's eternal identity. But McCormack's strategy for warding them off rests on a faulty assumption. McCormack believes that it offends against the nature of the living God to specify who God is apart from God's decision to be for us in the economy of salvation. McCormack concedes that Christians must be able to say that "God would be God without us" to preserve the gratuity of God's grace. Nevertheless, he maintains that Christians should refrain from trying "to specify precisely what God would be without us," on pain of obscuring God's revealed identity with "metaphysical speculation."[15] I think this gets things backward. The unwarranted bit of metaphysical spec-ulation is the assumption that the biblically attested God cannot reveal God's eternal identity as this "exists" antecedent to the deci-sion to elect. The Bible does exactly this in its portrait of God as the bearer of the Tetragrammaton. God does not need to be the Creator or "the God of Israel" to be the bearer of this name. The Tetragram-maton and "the God of Israel" are not synonyms. God is the *living* God precisely because God bears the Tetragrammaton irrespective of God's decision to be the God of Israel. This is the foundation of everything for which Israel gives YHWH praise. Affirming this has nothing to do with metaphysical speculation of any sort, ancient or modern. It has to do with harkening to the voice of the burning bush, which distinguishes with all clarity between "I am who I am" and "I am has sent me to you" (Exod 3:14). What makes the Bible a book of good news is that both names describe the same God: the LORD, the God of Abraham, of Isaac, and of Jacob (Exod 3:15).

In my opinion, the relevant counterfactual question is not "Would God be God without us?" but rather "Would YHWH be YHWH without us?" The former question is of no interest to the Bible. The latter is one the Bible positively demands that we ask. The difficulty with McCormack's position is that it does not permit an acceptable answer either way. If we say (as I believe we should), "Of course YHWH would be YHWH without us!" then we must abandon McCormack's claim that we cannot specify the identity of the biblical God apart from God's decision to be "for us and for our salvation." But if we cleave to that premise by saying, "YHWH would be *God* without us, but then God would not be YHWH," then we posit a deity antecedent to YHWH, the very thing the Bible is at pains to prohibit. This would be to engage in mythology and metaphysical speculation at once. It would reanimate a conception of God as the un- and underdetermined *X* whose banishment from Christian theology was the animating purpose of McCormack's position in the first place.

What then should we want to say? With George Hunsinger, we should say that it is possible to speak meaningfully about who the second person of the Trinity is prior to and apart from the decision to bear the name "Jesus Christ." Yet with Bruce McCormack, we should want to speak about the eternal second person in a way that leans maximally on the unsubstitutable specificity of the personal proper name "Jesus Christ." We do both things simultaneously when we supplement our talk about the eternal Trinity *by drawing on the pattern of naming the Trinity that orbits the unspoken Tetragrammaton.* "Before" the second person of the Trinity is Jesus Christ, the second person is the eternal Son, the eternal Word of God, *and* the eternal receiver of "the name above that is every name" (Phil 2:9). Jesus of Nazareth is *Ye-shua,* "the LORD is Salvation," because he is first of all in eternity the LORD.

Why Doesn't the Tetragrammaton Play a Role in Barth's Doctrine of Election?

In the remainder of this chapter, I want to take up a puzzle that has hovered in the background of our discussion. I pointed out that Barth claimed in part 1 of *Church Dogmatics*, volume 1, that the doctrine of the Trinity "does not seek to be anything but an explanatory confirmation" of the name *Yahweh-Kyrios*.[16] Nevertheless, the name is completely absent from Barth's doctrine of election in part 2 of *Church Dogmatics*, volume 2. Why is that? If the Tetragrammaton was foundational for Barth's doctrine of the Trinity, why did he not accord it a role in his doctrine of election?

To answer this question, we must turn to Barth's multifaceted doctrine of Israel.[17] Barth was a lifelong opponent of the idea that God rejected the Jews because they rejected the gospel, an idea we earlier called punitive supersessionism. Barth's rejection of punitive supersessionism was a great achievement in its time, and one for which his doctrine of Israel is justly honored today. But Barth's relationship to economic supersessionism and to "Israel/Tetragrammaton-forgetfulness" is more complex, and it is these features of his doctrine of Israel I want to examine now.

To recall an earlier chapter, "Israel-forgetfulness" arises when Christians conceive the standard canonical narrative in a way that makes the bulk of the Hebrew Scriptures indecisive for understanding the Trinity's eternal identity and the Trinity's works as Creator, Redeemer, and Consummator. There can be no doubt that by the time Barth began writing *Church Dogmatics*, his programmatic intention was to banish Israel-forgetfulness once and for all. Barth's determination on this score was crystallized by his love-hate relationship with Friedrich Schleiermacher, who had elevated Israel-forgetfulness to a matter of dogmatic principle a century earlier. Schleiermacher, it seems, provoked Barth to overcome Israel-forgetfulness with the same degree of intentionality. In his *Church Dogmatics*, Barth self-consciously makes God's covenant with Israel constitutive for how Christians understand the standard canonical narrative generally and God's reconciling action in Jesus Christ in particular.

Barth did not arrive at this resolve all at once. An index of how Barth's views evolved is provided by his changing understanding of the word *Lord*. Several years before Barth began writing *Church Dogmatics*, he had already unveiled his famous thesis that "God reveals himself as Lord" is the "root" of the doctrine of the Trinity. The claim appeared in Barth's first, abortive run at a multivolume dogmatics, *Christian Dogmatics*. But what does *Lord* (*kyrios*) mean? In an important discussion in the *Christian Dogmatics*, Barth explains that biblical scholars of the day were divided. Some maintained that *kyrios* was "a translation of the Old Testament name of God *Jahweh*," while others held that it was "the fervent trumping of everything which the world of Hellenistic religion worshiped in the way of gods, half gods . . . lords, and lordships." Barth concludes that it doesn't matter which of these options one chooses. Either way, *kyrios* means the same thing: "In either case, [*kyrios*] means a reality that one conceives personalistically, before which one bows in awe, thanksgiving, love, trust, petition, obedience. . . . One bows before the Lord, because the quintessence of superiority, power, and dignity is present in Him."[18]

At this point in his career, Barth thinks *Lord* gets its meaning from the existential encounter between God and humanity. So long as this is perceived, it is a matter of indifference whether one traces it back to "the Old Testament name of God."

Barth seems to have begun to have second thoughts shortly after *Christian Dogmatics* appeared in print. The book encountered a barrage of withering criticism. Barth had castigated others for erecting their concepts of the Trinity on common experience (the notorious *vestigia trinitatis*, or traces of the Trinity, that Barth accused of leading theology astray). But what was Barth's own thesis that "God reveals himself as Lord" other than his own *vestigium trinitatis* (trace of the Trinity), birthed by German idealism and left on the Bible's doorstep? Barth evidently felt the justice of the criticisms, and he abandoned *Christian Dogmatics* as a false start.

Several years later, Barth published a new account of the doctrine of the Trinity in the first volume of *Church Dogmatics*. He sticks to the thesis that the root of the doctrine is the affirmation "God reveals himself as Lord." But now Barth declares that this "root" actually rests on something yet deeper: "the revealed name *Yahweh-Kyrios*." The entire doctrine of the Trinity, Barth now urges, is nothing more or less than an "explanatory confirmation" of this name.[19] Barth, it seems, has made a major discovery: the importance of the Tetragrammaton for the biblical portrait of God. He has broken through the tradition's Tetragrammaton-amnesia, and now Schleiermacher's Israel-forgetfulness must be banished as well.

Barth's intention is clear. He means to ground the Christian conception of the keystone of the standard canonical narrative—the doctrine of the Trinity—on the specificity of the Bible's portrait of God, and not on human experience generally, as Schleiermacher had done. Barth also seems to realize, as he previously did not, the singular role that the Tetragrammaton plays in signaling the uniqueness of the biblical God. That is the insight that I have urged throughout this chapter. And yet, as I have already noted, a strange thing happens to the name *Yahweh-Kyrios* when Barth turns from the doctrine of the Trinity in volume 1 to the doctrine of election in volume 2. It vanishes. Tetragrammaton-amnesia strikes back.

To understand what happens to the Tetragrammaton, we must consider Barth's relationship to *economic* supersessionism. Economic supersessionism interprets the relationship of the Old Testament and the New according to the algorithm of promise, fulfillment, and *replacement*. It is the last member of this triad that is problematic. Economic supersessionism maintains that God elected Israel for the purpose of preparing for the coming of Christ and that Christ in turn renders the distinctive features of God's covenant with Israel *obsolete*. In brief, economic supersessionism implies that God wanted Jesus to be the last Jew.

Barth's posture toward economic supersessionism was quite different from his posture toward punitive supersessionism. While

Barth wholly rejected punitive supersessionism, he enthusiastically endorsed economic supersessionism. This is evident from the following passage from part 2 of *Church Dogmatics*, volume 1: "The king, the priest, the Law, sacrifice, the tabernacle, the temple, the holy land: all of them have to be assessed as a coherent group of signs pointing to a common center. But, of course, we have also to see a sign—the sign, as it were, of the superiority and freedom of the thing signified as compared with any of the signs—in the fact that this whole world of Old Testament signs disappears, so to speak, in a flash at the manifestation of Christ."[20]

It would be hard to find a more vivid and succinct statement of the logic of economic supersessionism in the whole history of Christian thought. Nor does Barth shy away from the implication that God wanted Jesus to be the last Jew. In a later volume of *Dogmatics*, he wrote, "The first Israel, constituted on the basis of physical descent from Abraham, has fulfilled its mission now that the Savior of the world has sprung from it and its Messiah has appeared. Its members can only accept this fact with gratitude, and in confirmation of their own deepest election and calling attach themselves to the people of this Savior, their own King, whose members the Gentiles are now called to be as well. *Its mission as a natural community has now run its course and cannot be continued or repeated.*"[21]

True, Barth does not quite say that the "natural community" *itself* "cannot be continued or repeated." Rather, what expires is its "mission" and all the God-given signs that differentiate it from the nations. But of course, the expiration of the one necessarily entails the expiration of the other. This is economic supersessionism with a vengeance.

At this point, we can anticipate how Tetragrammaton-amnesia is plotting its revenge. If economic supersessionism can "capture" the Tetragrammaton, bring it under the spell of its logic, then the Tetragrammaton too must "disappear in a flash," together with the world of signs that adorn and define the people descended from Abraham. If, on the other hand, the Tetragrammaton can evade capture by economic supersessionism, if Barth can imagine securing it a place *inside* the eternal identity of the Trinity, then the Tetragrammaton could subject economic supersessionism itself to interrogation. Standing outside the logic of promise, fulfillment, and cancelation, the Tetragrammaton could suggest another way of understanding Christ's relationship to the Old Testament's world of signs: promise, fulfillment, and *confirmation* (cf. 2 Cor 1:20).

But this is not what happens. In fact, economic supersessionism does capture Barth's understanding of the Tetragrammaton, and it does "disappear in a flash." Economic supersessionism's logic of promise, fulfillment, and cancelation requires that the Tetragrammaton be replaced by a superior name, and this is exactly what Barth maintains: "Into the place ... of the name of Yahweh that in the end really dwells in Jerusalem in a house of stone—there now comes the existence of the man Jesus of Nazareth, 'My Lord and my God.'"[22]

Barth did not come up with the idea that the Tetragrammaton is an "Old Testament name" that is replaced by a superior New Testament equivalent. The idea was first proposed in the late medieval period by the so-called Christian kabbalists and was later enthusiastically adopted by theologians from Luther to Hegel. According to one strand of this tradition, the name that replaces the Tetragrammaton is "Jesus." This is the strand that Barth takes up while giving it a slight existentialist twist: the Divine Name is replaced by Jesus's "existence." But since Jesus's existence is denoted by Jesus's name, Barth can adopt the more traditional view too. As he writes a few sentences later, the name "Yahweh" is replaced by "the historical figure of this Man on his way from Bethlehem to Golgotha, the 'name' of *Jesus*."[23]

Barth is ordinarily an astute exegete, but here the Christian kabbalists have led him astray. It is true that some New Testament texts suggest that Jesus takes the place of the temple in Jerusalem. *But what Jesus replaces is the house of stone and not the name that dwells there!* (cf. Matt 23:21). As the Fourth Gospel clearly maintains, Jesus himself is the fleshly temple of the Divine Name (John 2:19–21).

We can now see why Barth's "discovery" of the Tetragram-maton in his doctrine of the Trinity bears no fruit in his doctrine of election. Barth's warm embrace of economic supersessionism permitted it to capture his interpretation of the Tetragrammaton, thereby divorcing it from its proper place in the eternal Trinity and confining its significance to the Old Testament. Barth's thesis that "Jesus Christ is the electing God" was a brilliant overcorrection, an effort to plug a hole in the doctrine of God for which he himself was partly responsible. And it helps account for the sangfroid with which Barth can suggest that the electing God wanted Jesus to be the last Jew.

Covenant, Christ, Church

❦ 4 ❧

COVENANT

WHY DID GOD CHOOSE THE JEWS?

But now thus says the LORD,
he who created you, O Jacob,
he who formed you, O Israel:
Do not fear, for I have redeemed you;
I have called you by name, you are mine. (Isa 43:1)

WHY DID GOD choose the Jews? The question as it stands is ambiguous. Understood one way, it asks why God happened to choose the Jews rather than some other people, such as the Babylonians or the Navaho. Understood another way, it asks to what end God chose the Jews—that is, what is the purpose of Israel's election. Of course, the two questions are related, like all issues in Christian theology. At a minimum, correct answers will not contradict each other. More ambitiously, one may hope that a sound answer to one question will illuminate and deepen our understanding of the other. Nevertheless, the two questions are not the same and need to be considered separately at first.

Why Did God Choose the Jews Rather Than Some Other People?

The first question might seem intolerably nosy were it not explicitly addressed by Scripture. Deuteronomy 7:6–8 reads, "For you are a people holy to the LORD your God. The LORD your God has chosen you out of all the peoples on the face of the earth to be his people, his treasured possession. The LORD did not set his affection on you and choose you because you were more numerous than other peoples, for you were the fewest of all peoples. But it was because the Lord loved you and kept the oath he swore to your ancestors" (NIV).

The passage states that God chose Israel rather than some other people simply because "the Lord loved [Israel]" and kept faith with promises made to her ancestors (cf. Deut 8:17–18; 9:4–6; Hos 11:1; etc.). The answer is one that Christian authors have frequently endorsed in both academic and popular texts.[1] Writing for a general audience, David Pawson puts the matter this way: "'Why did God choose the Jews?' . . . Why not the Assyrians, the Greeks, the Ethiopians or the Chinese? Are the Jews more attractive, more reliable, more religious? Have they some unique racial qualities denied to all the other nations? I do not think so. God gives his reason for choosing the Jews in chapter seven of Deuteronomy. 'Do you think I love you because you are a greater nation than all the others? No, I love you *because I love you*.' That is the answer; and it lies not in them at all, but in him."[2]

Jewish tradition offers several possible answers to the same question. One explanation is that the Jews were chosen because their ancestor, Abraham, was the first person to recognize and accept the one God. Another explanation says that God offered the Torah to several other nations before offering it to the Jews, but they all refused, whereas Israel accepted.[3] Nevertheless, Jewish writers often settle on the same answer as Christians. Michael Wyschogrod consistently traces God's election of Israel back to the mystery of God's free and sovereign love for Abraham and his chosen descendants.[4] David Novak maintains that "the election of Israel is not due to any inherent properties, either biological (with their racist implications) or cultural (with their chauvinistic implications), by which Jews can claim to be inherently superior to the rest of humankind." Rather, God's choice of Israel is simply a matter of "divine grace or charity."[5]

To be sure, this answer only gets one so far. One could still wonder why God's spontaneous love happened to light on Abraham and his lineage rather than someone else and theirs. To this, the answer offers little recourse beyond an appeal to Augustinian caution: "It is better not to judge, unless you want to err."[6] Yet arguably, in this case, explanatory poverty is a feature, not a bug. The point the answer makes is that there is no humanly available answer beyond the inexplicable mystery of divine love itself.

To What End Did God Choose the Jews?

The previous question has a retrospective character: of all the people and lineages God might have chosen, why did God choose Abraham and his? The present question, in contrast, has a prospective orientation. Given that God did in fact choose the Jews, to what end did God do so? What is the purpose of Israel's election in God's economy of salvation? Here again, the Christian and Jewish traditions have answered the question in ways that partially overlap. Both traditions frequently connect God's purpose in calling Abraham and his descendants to God's redemptive purpose for humankind in a fallen and fractured world. But the traditions make this connection in characteristically different ways. The Jewish tradition anchors the purpose of Israel's election in God's gift of the Torah to Israel and in the unique relationship between God and Israel that the Torah makes possible. In contrast, the Christian tradition anchors the purpose of Israel's election in God's sending of the Messiah, Jesus Christ, and in the relationship between God and humanity that the Messiah makes possible.

I will return to Jewish reflections on the purpose of Israel's election later in this chapter. For now, I want to focus on Christian answers to the second question. Recently, Roy Schoeman has written that from a Roman Catholic perspective, God's purpose in electing the Jews is "actually quite straightforward":

> When man was first created, he was to live in a state of uninterrupted bliss and intimacy with God for all eternity. When Adam sinned, that initial state was shattered, and from that very moment—actually, even before then,

since God is outside time—God knew that He would someday restore man to an even higher state through the future incarnation of the second person of the most Holy Trinity as a man. If the second person of the most Holy Trinity was to incarnate as a man, it would be at a particular point in time and among a particular, "chosen" people. That people have to be prepared over many centuries. First, they would have to be separated from all of the other tribes around them who worshiped fallen spirits—that is, demons—masquerading as gods ("The gods of the gentiles are demons"—Ps. 96). They would have to learn about and worship the one true God, the uncreated Creator of all that is. They would have to be taught about the creation and fall of man, the seriousness of sin, the need for redemption and the coming of a Redeemer. They would have to be taught to adhere to a sufficiently high moral code that the incarnation itself would not be a sacrilege. They would have to be given sufficient divine revelation to be able to recognize the Redeemer when he came, and to be able to spread knowledge of his redemption to the rest of the world after he died. Finally, they would have to prepare, over the generations, a virgin of such purity and holiness that she could give her flesh and blood to be the flesh and blood of the God-man (the Blessed Virgin Mary). *That was the role for which the Jews were chosen*, and at which they succeeded, despite their widespread failure to follow him.[7]

While I do not subscribe to every detail of Schoeman's answer, I believe that it has several sound features. These include its emphasis on God's identity as the Holy Trinity, the centrality of the incarnation to God's redemptive purpose for fallen humankind, and the indispensable role that God's election of Israel plays in preparing for the coming of the Messiah, a role that includes providing the community into which the Messiah was born and the mother who gave him birth.

Having registered my general agreement with these aspects of Schoeman's answer, however, I want to draw attention to a difficulty that it presents for Christian theology. The account implies that Israel serves as the means to an end: the coming of the Messiah. It also implies that once the Messiah has come, Israel has no further reason to exist (though Schoeman himself does not draw that conclusion). These two ideas are clearly consistent with each other; moreover, they fit neatly into the narrative context of creation, fall, and redemption that Schoeman briefly sketches. Nevertheless, it is not immediately obvious how these ideas can be consistent with the claim that God chose Israel because "the LORD loved [Israel]" (cf. Deut 7:6–8). As Joel Kaminsky has observed, "Love relationships are not best conceived in instrumental terms, especially a love relationship like that between God and Israel."[8] And surely the incongruity that Kaminsky identifies becomes even starker if we imagine that God chose to love Israel with an expiration date in mind.

To be clear, I do not think that the difficulty I just identified is particular to Schoeman's account of the purpose of Israel's election; rather, it arises in connection with any Christian account that shares its general shape, which is to say, the great majority of them. Admittedly, it is easy to make the difficulty disappear. All one has to do is reject the idea that God really loved Israel in a special way in the first place. But such a refusal raises problems of coherence of its own, given the fact that both Old and New Testaments testify so extensively to the contrary. To illustrate how hard it is to make good sense of the Bible while denying that Israel is God's especially beloved people, we will examine a work by the Old Testament scholar and missiologist Christopher J. H. Wright.

C. H. J. Wright on the Purpose of YHWH's Election of Israel: An Instrumental View

In his almost six-hundred-page book *The Mission of God: Unlocking the Bible's Grand Narrative*, Christopher Wright offers a richly detailed account of the Bible's "grand metanarrative" (63), which he hopes will provide a platform for a "missional" understanding of the church today.[9] The hermeneutical key to unlocking the Bible's grand narrative, Wright maintains, is "the mission of God," which he defines as "God's will to be known by his whole creation" (473), or, more succinctly, as "the blessing of the nations" (178). The plot complication that motivates God's mission is the sin and rebellion of the human race, which the Bible narrates in Genesis 3–11. God's mission itself commences with Genesis 12 and God's covenant with Abraham, which generates "a vast, arching trajectory that carries from Genesis 12 to Revelation 22" (189). The center and pivot of God's mission is God's sending of his Son, Jesus Christ. Everything in the Bible either "leads *up* to Christ" or "leads *on from* Christ" (41). The Bible culminates with a vision of a future time when God's will to be known by creation is accomplished at last and God's mission is complete.

A noteworthy feature of Wright's account of the grand narrative of the Bible is the strong emphasis that he puts on God's personal proper name "YHWH." Following Richard Bauckham, Wright maintains that the name YHWH signifies the "transcendent uniqueness" of the biblical Deity.[10] Whereas mere uniqueness is sufficient to distinguish one member of a class from other members of it, the name YHWH signifies that God's uniqueness transcends everything else and "puts YHWH in a class of his own" (82). The marks of YHWH's transcendent uniqueness include YHWH's incomparability, identity as the Creator of all things, and sovereignty over history. These marks of YHWH's identity are directly relevant to understanding the nature of God's mission, for God's mission is nothing other than YHWH's desire to be known by all creation as the transcendentally unique God that YHWH is.

Another noteworthy feature of Wright's account of the Bible's metanarrative is the detailed treatment he accords to the Old Testament's testimony to YHWH's election of Israel. Following the precedent that Augustine set in his work *The Trinity*, Christian theologians have sometimes maintained that God did not inaugurate God's mission prior to God's sending of the Son in the incarnation and the Holy Spirit on the day of Pentecost. In this view, the Old Testament does not actually contain a record of God's mission. Rather, it foreshadows God's future mission, which is recorded by the New Testament. This understanding of God's mission, in turn, has made it natural for some Christians (though not for Augustine himself) to think in terms of an "abridged" version of the Bible's grand narrative that leaps directly from Genesis 1–3 to the New Testament while dispensing with most of the Old Testament. Wright certainly does not do this. On the contrary, he maintains that YHWH inaugurated YHWH's mission of salvation by calling Abraham (Gen 12), and he devotes lavishly detailed attention to the covenant between YHWH and Abraham's chosen descendants, the people Israel.

At the same time, Wright has a very particular understanding of the role that YHWH intended Israel to play in the Bible's grand narrative. YHWH chose Israel to be the instrument that YHWH uses to make himself known to the nations and to bless the nations. "*The election of Israel is instrumental,*" he writes with emphasis, "*not an end in itself*" (263; italics original). Wright thinks this point so crucial for the logic of the Bible's grand narrative that he makes it repeatedly, frequently using italics for emphasis:

> "There is a teleological (purposeful) thrust to Israel's existence.... Ultimately, Israel existed *for the sake of the nations.*" (57; italics original)
> "Israel came into existence as a people with a mission entrusted to them from God for the sake of God's wider purpose for blessing the nations." (65)
> "God [was] so determined to bless the nations that he chose Abraham." (134)

> "*Blessing for the nations is the bottom line, textually and theologically, of God's promise to Abraham.*" (194; italics original)

> "The ingathering of the nations was the very thing Israel existed for in the purpose of God; it was the fulfilment of the bottom line of God's promise to Abraham." (194)

> "*Israel knew God in order that through them all nations would come to know God.*" (262; italics original)

I suggested earlier that a tension exists between the affirmation that God chose the Jews out of spontaneous love for them and the affirmation that God chose the Jews as a means to an end. Wright's book provides an opportunity to test this thesis. If a tension really exists, then we should expect it to be difficult for Wright to affirm that YHWH has a special love for Israel for her own sake. And in fact, such affirmations are exceedingly rare in Wright's massive book, if not totally nonexistent. Of course, references to YHWH's love are plentiful, and many of these occur in close proximity to the name "Israel." On careful examination, however, the sentences in question never say what a casual reader might suppose them to say. An example is the passage that appears immediately prior to Wright's (italicized) claim that "*the election of Israel is instrumental, not an end in itself.*" There Wright writes, "*The election of Israel is founded only on God's inexplicable love.* There was no other motive than God's own love, and the promises he made to Israel's forefathers (which included, of course, his promise in relation to the nations). We might paraphrase John 3:16, in a way that John would doubtless accept, 'God so loved *the world* that he chose Abraham and called Israel'" (263; italics original).

The casual reader might suppose that Wright is making an affirmation similar to the paraphrase of Deuteronomy 7:6–8 that I cited earlier by David Pawson: "I love you *because I love you.*" But Wright is saying no such thing. Wright says that "God's inexplicable love" is the *foundation* of the election of Israel but not that it was directed *toward* Israel. Nor does Wright say that in the following two sentences. God's inexplicable love is the motive that lies behind God's election of Israel and God's promises to the patriarchs, but the object of God's love is *the world*, not Israel. What Wright carefully refrains from saying throughout is that "God's inexplicable love" was for Israel herself.

Once one notices this feature of Wright's text, one can confirm that it shapes his account of "the Bible's grand narrative" from beginning to end. I wrote a moment ago that affirmations of YHWH's special love for Israel are virtually nonexistent in Wright's text. That is not entirely true. The Bible contains dozens of such passages, and while Wright generally avoids citing the most explicit of these (e.g., Deut 4:37; 1 Kgs 10:9; Isa 43:1; 49:14–16; Hos 3:1; etc.), occasionally, one appears in the pages of his book and makes the affirmation for him. An example is this passage from Deuteronomy, which Wright cites twice: "Although heaven and the heaven of heavens belong to the LORD your God, the earth with all that is in it, yet the LORD set his heart in love on your ancestors alone and chose you, their descendants after them, out of all the peoples, as it is today" (Deut 10:14–15).

On the first occasion that Wright cites this passage, he draws the following lesson: "Whatever else we may say about the election of Israel, it cannot be construed as narrow and exclusive favoritism that paid no attention to the wider world" (260). While this may be true, it can hardly be said to be the main point of the verse at hand, which is (obviously) that YHWH has a special love for Israel. The second time that Wright cites the passage, he does mention God's "condescending love in choosing Abraham and his descendants," but he immediately adds that God chose them "to be the special vehicle of his blessing" (364). Wright's instrumental gloss is completely gratuitous and lacks any basis in the text whatsoever. Wright adds it, we may safely presume, to ward off the verse's unwelcome implication that YHWH loves Israel for her own sake, a truth that is inconsistent with Wright's vision of the Bible's grand narrative.

Another way that Wright deflects the idea that YHWH has a special love for Israel is by arguing that YHWH's relationship to Israel is simply typical of how YHWH relates to everyone all the time anyway. This is how Wright interprets Israel's foundational saga, the exodus: "God was simply acting in character—doing for Israel what he typically does for others. That is what YHWH does for aliens generically. That is the kind of God he is. YHWH is the God who loves to love, and especially to love the needy and the alien. Since the Israelites were in that needy condition in Egypt, they became the objects of his compassionate justice" (80).

If this were really true, of course, it would be hard to explain why the Old Testament focuses so obsessively on YHWH's relationship to one particular people. Still, the expediency of the claim is obvious. It gives Wright a way to acknowledge that the Old Testament does in fact speak of YHWH's love for Israel while denying that there is anything extraordinary about this love. Wright interprets YHWH's entire relationship with Israel in the same vein: "The loving concern and redemptive action that God had demonstrated in the social arena of Israel's history, while they were unique within the framework of his covenantal relationship with them, were not exceptional and exclusive. Rather they were, in the proper sense, *typical.* That is simply how it is with YHWH God" (283; italics original).

In sum, Wright maintains that what makes YHWH's covenant with Israel unique is not that YHWH has a special love for Israel but rather that YHWH uses Israel as his chosen instrument to show the watching nations what kind of God YHWH truly is.

We have seen enough of Wright's account of Israel's place in the Bible's grand narrative to offer an assessment. One possible criticism is that it lays the groundwork for an account of the church's relationship to the Jewish people that is supersessionist—that is, that issues in the denial that the Jews are God's elect people. Such a criticism is certainly valid. Wright maintains that "the distinctiveness of Israel from the nations . . . was essential to the mission of God" prior to Christ's advent, but thereafter, it was essential that

Israel's distinctiveness "be dissolved" into the life of the church where the distinction between Jew and gentile is completely erased (500). Wright rejects the view that "Jews still have a valid covenantal relationship with God" apart from faith in Christ and maintains that "evangelism among the Jewish people" is a biblical imperative for gentile Christians (529). Nevertheless, I do not think that criticizing Wright on these grounds is very useful or interesting. For one thing, Wright does not claim to offer a Christian account of the Bible's grand narrative that is nonsupersessionist, and indeed, he would probably accept the charge of supersessionism as a badge of honor. For another, I have pointed out that a tendency toward supersessionism seems to go hand in hand with the Christian belief that God chose the Jews for a purpose that is connected to the advent of Jesus Christ, the Redeemer of the world. Seen in this light, Wright's remorselessly instrumental account of Israel's election merely illuminates a pitfall that confronts every Christian theologian, and especially those like myself who want to envision the church's standard canonical narrative in a nonsupersessionist way.

More illuminating, I think, are criticisms that assess Wright's proposal in light of criteria that he himself sets forth. One of these is "a hermeneutic of coherence," which requires that Wright's account of the Bible's grand narrative hang together as a plausible construal of the biblical data (41). I think that Wright's exclusively instrumental interpretation of Israel's election fails to meet that test. The problem with an exclusively instrumental interpretation of the Old Testament's testimony to YHWH's covenant with Israel is not merely that it leads to supersessionism, true though that is. The problem more basically is that it makes a hash of sacred Scripture. Far from being plausible, there is something almost cartoonish about Wright's effort to deflect the reader's attention from something that the Old Testament affirms so frequently: God loves Abraham and his chosen descendants in a special way that distinguishes them from every other people on earth. Wright's attention to the Tetragrammaton as the special sign of God's "transcendent uniqueness" is commendable, but in the context of his proposal, it serves merely to underscore the stark implausibility of an exclusively instrumental interpretation of YHWH's covenant with Israel.[11]

A second immanent criticism is that Wright's proposal fails to provide a sound platform for a missional understanding of the church. According to Wright, YHWH elected Israel to show the nations what kind of God YHWH is. He never seems to reflect on the fact that a god who uses god's chosen people in a purely instrumental way is unlikely to prove very attractive to anyone. A constant refrain of the literature of missiology and evangelism is that the mission of God in which Christians participate cannot be adequately conceived in functional, instrumental, and pragmatic terms alone. Effective mission and ministry are relational, not transactional. As the eminent missiologist Lesslie Newbigin observed many decades ago, "It is precisely because she [the church] is not merely instrumental that she can be instrumental." "The means by which the good news of salvation is propagated," Newbigin continues, "must be congruous with the nature of salvation itself."[12] Wright would have provided a sounder basis for a missional understanding of the church if he had recognized that the relevance of Newbigin's observation begins with the church's theology of Israel and the Jewish people. It is only if Christians first recognize that YHWH's love for Israel is not merely instrumental that they can plausibly maintain that God has assigned her an instrumental role in the blessing of the nations.

Finally, Wright's book provides occasion to direct an immanent criticism not to Wright but to myself. In the first chapter of this book, I advanced the thesis that supersessionism is a contingent distortion of the church's "standard canonical narrative" rather than a necessary feature of it. I also claimed that the key to envisioning the standard canonical narrative in a nonsupersessionist way is the recovery of the pancanonical significance of the Tetragrammaton as the singular name of God. *The Mission of God* seems to provide evidence that counts against my second claim in particular. As we have seen, Wright accords great significance to the Tetragrammaton in his reading of the Old Testament, and he does the same in his reading of the New, although we did not examine the latter aspect of his work. Nevertheless, his account of the Bible's grand narrative is explicitly and unapologetically supersessionist. At a minimum, his book demonstrates that awareness of the Tetragrammaton's pancanonical significance is not a panacea that automatically causes the standard canonical narrative to assume a nonsupersessionist shape. I therefore now want to reformulate my thesis in a more qualified form. An awareness of the Bible's pancanonical witness to the Tetragrammaton is a necessary but not sufficient condition for understanding the Bible's grand narrative in a nonsupersessionist way. A further condition is that the reader allow this witness to reshape their understanding of the Bible's grand narrative in ways that bring it into greater conformity with central features of God's identity as YHWH as attested by the canon as a whole. One such feature, I would submit, is that YHWH loves the people Israel in a special way that forever distinguishes her from every other people of the earth.

"I Have Called You by Name": Toward a Nonsupersessionist Account of the Purpose of Israel's Election

In the remainder of this chapter, I want to sketch a Christian understanding of the purpose of Israel's election that affirms both that that purpose is teleologically oriented to Jesus Christ, the ultimate ground of God's inexplicable love for everyone, and also that God loves Israel in a special way that forever distinguishes her from other peoples. My starting point is one prominent way that Jews have understood the purpose of their election. In their classic anthology of rabbinic literature, Claude Goldsmid Montefiore (a liberal Jew) and Herbert Loewe (an orthodox Jew) characterize the rabbinic understanding of the purpose of Israel's election in this way: "The purpose of Israel's election by God is that it shall sanctify God's name, and be a holy people dedicated to God's service."[13]

This definition differs from Christopher Wright's in an important way: it locates the purpose of Israel's election inside its own relationship to God. Israel's purpose is both to do something ("sanctify God's name") and to be something ("a holy people dedicated to God's service") in relation to YHWH. The primary orientation of the definition is vertical, although both clauses have horizontal implications. As Israel sanctifies God's name and exists as a holy people in God's service (vertical axis), it does so in a fallen and fractured world inhabited by the nations who may watch what is going on and draw their own conclusions (horizontal axis). Presumably, God may choose to assign high importance to the horizontal relationship between Israel and the nations, or even extremely high importance; nevertheless, it is not the primary axis of the purpose of Israel's election, which remains the vertical one between Israel and God. In contrast, Wright defines Israel's purpose in an exclusively horizontal fashion: Israel exists to bless the nations. Of course, Wright is aware that a vertical relationship exists between God and Israel, but when he mentions it in connection with the purpose of Israel's election, he subsumes it into the horizontal axis, as when he writes, *"Israel knew God in order that through them all nations would come to know God"* (262; italics original).

This first difference is closely related to a second one. The rabbis (as Montefiore and Loewe understand them) define the purpose of Israel's election with reference to two proper names, whereas Wright's definition has only one. According to rabbinic understanding, Israel's teleology has a proper name at each end of its vertical axis: YHWH above, Israel below. The rabbinic definition further underscores the importance of YHWH's proper name by making Israel's first task that of "sanctifying God's name" and making the task of being "a holy people dedicated to God's service" follow thereafter. In contrast, Wright defines the purpose of Israel's election without any reference to the Tetragrammaton at all. Israel exists to bless the nations. Israel's proper name remains, but it is not anchored in its own relationship to YHWH.

Significant implications flow from the fact that the rabbis, unlike Wright, define the purpose of Israel's election in terms of a relationship between subjects who are both identified by proper name (YHWH and Israel).[14] We use proper names for nonfungible objects: objects for which qualitative duplicates would be unacceptable. Proper names are not equally important in all kinds of relationships or in all kinds of literature. Aesop's fables, for example, are rich in character and incident but poor in proper names. This is not a criticism but an observation about the kind of literature it is and the kind of wisdom it is designed to convey. What matters is that on a certain occasion, a tortoise and a hare agreed to race, not that it was this particular tortoise and this particular hare. Occasionally, a fable relates an encounter between a god and mortals, and in such cases, the god is always identified by his or her proper name, for example, Hermes, Apollo, Aphrodite, and so on. But even in these stories, the mortal characters are still identified only as a fox, a raven, a cobbler, and so on. The nonfungibility of the god's identity, it seems, is such that it does not "rub off" on the mortal characters with whom they interact. Aesop's Hermes has an unsubstitutable identity, but Aesop's fox is still just a fox.

In contrast, the Bible portrays YHWH as a transcendent nonfungible being who can choose to make his nonfungibility "rub off" on those with whom he interacts, so that they too acquire unsubstitutable identities in their own right. Indeed, the Bible's insistence on YHWH's unsubstitutability is so vehement that it deserves to be included among the marks of YHWH's "transcendent uniqueness" (Bauckham), alongside YHWH's incomparability, sovereignty over history, and identity as the Creator of all things.[15] To identify God by means of the proper name YHWH is to signify not only that God is incomparable, sovereign, and the Creator of all things but that YHWH is all of these things in an utterly nonfungible way that is anchored in and announced by the name YHWH itself. Moreover, YHWH can choose to interact with his creatures in such a way that YHWH's nonfungibility rubs off on them too. This is what YHWH has in fact done by choosing Israel to be his people. That is the significance of the fact that the rabbis define the purpose of Israel's election with reference to two proper names: they define the poles of a relationship that, like the parties that constitute it, is unsubstitutable.

We can illustrate what it means to say that YHWH's nonfungibility rubs off on Israel by comparing two biblical stories. The book of Job informs us in its opening verses that in addition to many servants and livestock, Job had seven sons and three daughters, all of whom are dead by the end of the first chapter. At the end of the book, we learn that "the LORD restored the fortunes of Job" and that he was once again the happy father of seven sons and three daughters (Job 42:10). Not coincidentally, the story does not identify Job's first ten children by name. To have done so would have clouded the story's happy ending by drawing attention to the nonfungibility of the dead children. For the purposes of the story, being a child of Job is a role that many individuals can play. What matters is that Job got ten children back, not that he got any particular child back. In contrast, 2 Samuel portrays King David's relationship to the third of his twenty-one sons in a very different way. Upon learning of the miserable death of his beautiful, narcissistic child, David laments, "O my son Absalom, O Absalom, my son, my son!" (2 Sam 19:4). David has lost a child, but not just any child. David has lost Absalom. David's repeated use of Absalom's proper name underscores the irreplaceability of the child who is gone.

Zooming out, we may ask which of these two stories the Old Testament's global portrait of YHWH's relationship to the people Israel more closely resembles. The answer is obvious: the one with two proper names, the story of David and Absalom. This answer is required not only to account for YHWH's repeated expressions of love for Israel but also for YHWH's expressions of anger, grief, and even regret toward her. An example is this verse from Jeremiah, which I cite here according to the King James Version for the sake of its exquisite translation: "Is Ephraim my dear son? is he a pleasant child? for since I spake against him, I do earnestly remember him still: therefore my bowels are troubled for him; I will surely have mercy upon him, saith the LORD" (Jer 31:20 KJV).

The same sense of the unsubstitutability of the object of YHWH's affection informs Jesus's anguished lament for Jerusalem (Matt 23:37-39) and Paul's "great sorrow and unceasing anguish" (Rom 9:2) on behalf of his "kindred according to the flesh" (Rom 9:3) in Romans 9–11. Jesus and Paul participate in YHWH's love for an irreplaceable child. Christopher Wright's account of the Bible's grand narrative lacks any appreciation for the unsubstitutability of Israel in YHWH's affections, and it is this that makes it so unpersuasive. Wright does cite the verse from Jeremiah quoted in the previous paragraph, but he does so in support of the claim that the purpose of the exodus is for YHWH to make a great name "among the nations." While this is true enough, the relevance of the observation to Jeremiah 31:20 is hard to see. One might as well say that the purpose of David's grief for Absalom is to shore up his political support. (In fact, it has the opposite effect.)

A fascinating feature of the biblical narrative is that early on, it explicitly probes the question of whether the people Israel really occupies a nonfungible place in relation to YHWH and, if so, why. The incident of the golden calf represents Israel's remarkably speedy and utterly wholesale failure to fulfill its vocation to sanctify YHWH's name and to be a holy people in his service. YHWH's initial response to the crisis is the obvious one—replace Israel with a different people that will better serve God's purposes: "I have seen this people, how stiff-necked they are. Now let me alone, so that my wrath may burn hot against them and I may consume them; and of you [Moses] I will make a great nation" (Exod 32:9–10).

Not surprisingly, the story has appealed to Christians who claim that there is no irrevocable link between God's desire to have a people and the Jewish people per se. *The Epistle of Barnabas* (ca. 100 CE) cites the incident of the golden calf to demonstrate that God broke the covenant with Israel shortly after making it and that it is a sin for Christians to say that "the covenant is both theirs and ours" (*Barnabas* 4). But Barnabas ignores what happens next. Before YHWH can execute the switch, Moses intercedes:

> O LORD, why does your wrath burn hot against your people, whom you brought out of the land of Egypt with great power and with a mighty hand? Why should the Egyptians say, "It was with evil intent that he brought them out to kill them in the mountains, and to consume them from the face of the earth"? Turn from your fierce wrath; change your mind and do not bring disaster on your people. Remember Abraham, Isaac, and Israel, your servants, how you swore to them by your own self, saying to them, "I will multiply your descendants like the stars of heaven, and all this land that I have promised I will give to your descendants, and they shall inherit it forever." (Exod 32:11–13)

Moses urges two considerations. If God destroys Israel, the gentiles will talk and God's reputation will suffer. Furthermore, Moses reminds God that the oath God swore to "Abraham, Isaac, and Israel, [God's] servants" was solemnized with reference to "[God's] own self." In effect, Moses is telling YHWH that it's too late to replace Israel with another people. By swearing an oath to Israel by "[God's] own self," YHWH has made relationship to this particular people an internal aspect of YHWH's self-relation. The issue is no longer just a matter of how loving YHWH may be feeling toward Israel at any particular time, or how serviceable Israel proves to be as a people dedicated to God's service, or even (God forbid) what the nations will say. The issue is whether YHWH will be true to his own transcendent uniqueness as God. YHWH has already allowed his name to rub off on Israel. Now even YHWH can't erase the mark without profaning his own name.

The force of Moses's reasoning echoes through the canon. It proves persuasive to YHWH on the occasion of the incident of the golden calf, and the prophets record how God subsequently adopts it into his own reasoning when talking back to Israel: "Thus says the Lord God: It is not for your sake, O house of Israel, that I am about to act, but for the sake of my holy name, which you have profaned among the nations to which you came. I will sanctify my great name, which has been profaned among the nations, and which you have profaned among them; and the nations shall know that I am the Lord, says the Lord God, *when through you I display my holiness before their eyes*" (Ezek 36:22–23; italics added).

God is definitely concerned with sanctifying God's name in the eyes of the nations, but the only way God can do that is by honoring the nonfungible status that God accorded to the people that God chose. What will prove so amazing to the nations is that God's relationship with Israel will become what God intended it to be. The oracle continues, "I will put my spirit within you, and make you follow my statutes and be careful to observe my ordinances. Then you shall live in the land that I gave to your ancestors; and you shall be my people, and I will be your God" (Ezek 36:27–28).

As important as it is, YHWH's status among the nations remains a reflex of YHWH's relationship to Israel, which remains the primary axis along which YHWH must demonstrate the holiness of God's name. If Israel does not do its part to sanctify God's name, God will solve the problem by sanctifying his own name on their behalf, for his own name's sake. God will do this not by replacing Israel with another people but by taking the initiative to forgive and restore the irreplaceable child who has stumbled but not fallen for good.

It is this same line of reasoning that informs Paul's reflections in Romans 9–11 on the covenantal status of the great majority of his kinsmen who have not accepted the gospel of Jesus Christ. Paul begins the section by affirming that his fellow Jews who have not recognized Jesus as Messiah "*are* Israelites" (present tense) and that to them belong "the adoption, the glory, the covenants, the giving of the law, the worship, and the promises" (Rom 9:4). Paul then subjects his kinsmen to withering criticism for much of the next three chapters for failing to submit to "God's righteousness" in Christ (Rom 10:3–4). Nevertheless, Paul ends the section by concluding that "as regards election they are beloved, for the sake of their ancestors; for the gifts and the calling of God are irrevocable" (Rom 11:28–29). Unsurprisingly, these last verses are missing from the Scripture index of Wright's book.

We can extend the present line of investigation by returning to the question, Why did God choose the Jews rather than some other people? As we saw at the beginning of this chapter, both Christians and Jews have answered the question by pointing to God's inexplicable love. But we can now make this answer more precise by recalling some basic features of the biblical story. It is not the case that the YHWH's love happened to light on a people that already bore the name "Israel" independently of YHWH's previous action. The LORD's choice of Israel was not like that of the featured bachelor on a game show who selects a date named Naomi from among several eligible contestants. Rather, the people named Israel comes into existence because the LORD first called Abram and Sarai by name and made a promise to them, which he then subsequently fulfilled. The LORD's inexplicable love *creates* Israel by calling it by name:

> But now thus says the LORD,
> he who created you, O Jacob,
> he who formed you, O Israel:
> Do not fear, for I have redeemed you;
> I have called you by name, you are mine. (Isa 43:1)

The question Why did God choose the Jews rather than some other people? actually resolves into the question Why did God call the Jews into existence by proper name rather than some other people? The answer remains the same as before—God's mysterious love—but we are now in a position to better gauge the full depth of that love, which "calls into existence the things that do not exist" (Rom 4:17).

We are also better able to understand why God's calling of Israel is accompanied by God's gift to her of the Torah and why the *kind* of people the Jews are is so difficult to adequately determine. By calling the community of Israel into existence by name, God bestows on this people a nonfungible identity, one that is a very distant likeness of YHWH's own nonfungible identity, traced in the medium of frail and fallen human flesh. God's gift of the Torah gives Israel's nonfungible identity lasting shape in the world and is therefore constitutive of Israel's existence for all time (cf. Paul's use of the present tense to describe "the covenants, the giving of the law, the worship" in Rom 9:4). The Torah applies the gift of "being called by name" to every nook and cranny of Israel's existence; that is why the names "YHWH" and "Israel" occur so ubiquitously in the book of Leviticus (1:2, 4:2, 4:13, 7:29, 7:36, 7:38, etc.). Furthermore, because YHWH is transcendently unique, the people on whom he has chosen to have his name rub off is also unique, albeit in a distant, derivative, and imperfect way (cf. Exod 33:16). The sense in which the Jewish people is *a people* is sui generis, bearing some resemblance to and yet not coinciding with any general classification, whether family, tribe, confederation, nation, people, lineage, ethnicity, culture, and so on. Israel's identity is nonfungible but not inflexible, having borne greater or lesser resemblance to many of these categories at different times while never settling down permanently in any of them.[16]

These considerations, in turn, illuminate the relationships that exist between God, Israel, and the nations even prior to taking up the question, To what end did God choose the Jews? According to Christian understanding, God's inexplicable love in Christ is directed to all the children of Adam from before the foundation of the world, to Jew and gentile alike.[17] Nevertheless, God's inexplicable love for Israel takes a special shape that forever differentiates her from all other families, peoples, tribes, nations, and lineages. *Only Israel exists as a family/people/tribe/nation/lineage that God has called into being by name and that God has chosen to relate to by name.* To be born a Jew is to be born into a human lineage with a proper name assigned to it by the explicit, authoritative Word of God; to become a Jew means to be adopted into this same lineage. No gentile is born into a lineage of this sort, nor can they acquire a lineage of this sort except by becoming Jews. As creatures made in the image of God, gentiles are endowed no less than Jews with nonfungible identities, with what Kierkegaard called a "name divinely understood."[18] Gentiles, no less than Jews, come into the world called and surrounded by God's inexplicable love. But that love operates among gentiles in ways other than by means of God's authoritative word that names and claims the communities to which they belong. Nor does the church exist in the same way that Israel does. The church is the body of Christ, who is the incarnate Word of God and the Redeemer of Jew and gentile alike. But *church* (*ekklesia*) is not a proper name, nor is the church a human *lineage* of any sort. Tertullian was correct: Christians are made, not born. Jews and gentiles who are baptized into Christ are "born from above" (John 3:3). They are united to Christ and to one another in a new spiritual kinship group that shares Jesus's filial address to God and that is a foretaste of the new creation. But Jews who are baptized do not thereby lose their status as members of God's chosen people, however irregular and defective this status becomes in the view of historic Judaism. Nor do gentiles who are baptized cease to be gentiles—that is, people who herald from and continue to participate in human communities that God has *not* called by name. Contra Wright, the New Testament's portrait of the ecclesial unity of Jew and gentile preserves the distinction between them (Acts 15), just as it portrays the distinction between Israel and the nations as a recognizable feature of the new creation (cf. Rev 7:4–8, 21:24, 26).

We are now ready to return to the question, To what end did God choose the Jews? As we have seen over the course of this chapter, this is a challenging question for Christians to answer in a nonsupersessionist way because a tension seems to arise between two affirmations that Christians are obliged to make. On the one hand, Christians should want to affirm that YHWH called Israel into being by name because of God's inexplicable love *for her* (cf. Deut 7:6–8) and that YHWH's love for Israel and the gifts it confers are irrevocable (cf. Rom 11:29). This affirmation is obligatory for Christians both because it provides the best answer to the question Why did God choose the Jews rather than some other people? and because the plain sense of the Old and New Testaments requires it. On the other hand, Christians should want to affirm that YHWH called Israel into existence by name for the sake of Jesus Christ, the Savior of the world. This answer is obligatory for Christians because they understand Jesus Christ to be the unique and unsurpassable Savior of the world, the one in whom all the councils of God "hold together" (Col 1:17), and the wellspring of God's inexplicable love for Israel and the nations alike. Tension seems to arise between the statements because the more one stresses God's inexplicable love for Israel *as Israel*, the less satisfactory an emphasis on the instrumental purpose of their election becomes, whereas the more one stresses the instrumental purpose of their election, the less intelligible it becomes that God loves Israel as Israel. This tension is exacerbated by the fact that Christians naturally understand the instrumental purpose of Israel's election as oriented toward the incarnation of the eternal Word of God by the Virgin Mary, an event that has already happened, whereas God's love for Israel as Israel demands to be understood as "irrevocable"—that is, as coming with no "expiration date."

As a first step toward resolving this apparent tension, we can orient ourselves once again on Montefiore and Lowe's definition of the purpose of Israel's election, which is to "sanctify God's name, and be a holy people dedicated to God's service." We have already seen that while the primary axis of this definition is vertical, it does not rule out a horizontal dimension. What the definition rules out is the idea not that God employs Israel in God's service but rather that service exhausts the meaning of Israel's election. I noted earlier that Joel Kaminsky has written that "love relationships are not best conceived in instrumental terms, especially a love relationship like that between God and Israel." Yet while Kaminsky rejects an *instrumental* interpretation of Israel's election, he, like Montefiore and Lowe, affirms the idea that God's choice of Israel obligates her to divine *service*. In fact, Kaminsky goes so far as to say that "election reaches its greatest heights when the elect humbly submit to the divine service God has placed upon them." At the same time, Kaminsky cautions, Israel's election is "not reducible to service." Rather, "*it flows out of God's mysterious love for those chosen*" (italics added). These reflections suggest that we must draw a firm distinction between understanding Israel as God's *instrument* that God *uses* and understanding Israel as God's *beloved* whose *service* God requires. The difference is clear. Instruments are fungible; when a surgeon's scalpel is nicked, she throws it away and takes another. In contrast, the service provided by God's chosen is non-fungible because it is inseparable from "God's mysterious love for those chosen."[19] Clearly, only the second view is adequate for a Christian understanding of the purpose of Israel's election that seeks to be nonsupersessionist. Indeed, only the second view is adequate for any plausible interpretation of the Bible at all.

Yet we still face the task of illuminating what Israel's servant role is as this relates to Jesus Christ, the person whom Christians understand to be the source and center of God's mysterious love for everyone, chosen and unchosen alike. I believe the kernel of a fitting answer is found in the words of the angelic messenger who addressed Mary: "And now, you will conceive in your womb and bear a son, and you will name him Jesus" (Luke 1:31).

It is possible to read this verse in a way that puts the emphasis on its first half—that is, on Mary's role as the one who "could give her flesh and blood to be the flesh and blood of the God-man." This is where Roy Schoeman puts the emphasis in the passage I cited near the beginning of this chapter. To put the emphasis on this point is to stress the corporeality of the incarnation and, by extension, the corporeality of the people Israel, which provides the "flesh and blood" of the lineage from which Mary and the Messiah come. Michael Wyschogrod proposed a similar understanding of the incarnation, according to which Christian belief in the incarnation represents an "intensification" of Judaism's belief in God's indwelling among the people Israel.[20] While I do not think this understanding of what Israel/Mary gives to Jesus is false, I do not think it puts the emphasis in the right place. Rather, the most important thing that Israel/Mary gives to Jesus resides in her capacity to hear and obey the second half of the angel's message: "You will name him Jesus." Even before Jesus of Nazareth existed, God called him to be God's beloved child and to be God's servant—in that order. God called him by name to be the human being on whom God's own name "rubbed off" in a uniquely vivid and nonfungible way. In order for God to call Jesus in this way, God had to have previously called a people by name to be God's beloved child and servant—in that order. Only a people on whom God's name had already rubbed off, a people consecrated to the sanctification of God's name, a people beloved for its own sake, could serve God's saving purpose for the world by providing the community in which the Messiah's mother could hear and obey the command "You will name him Jesus."

When Christians understand the purpose of Israel's election in this way, the gulf that separates their understanding of Judaism from Judaism's self-understanding will not disappear. But it will be immediately evident to Christians why God's election of Israel comes with no expiration date. *It does so precisely because of its orientation to Jesus Christ.* Like the Messiah, the people from whom the Messiah comes bears the imprint of God's name irrevocably. That is certainly why Paul formulates the list of his kinsmen's privileges in the present tense, and why the list concludes in the striking way it does: "They are Israelites, and to them belong the adoption, the glory, the covenants, the giving of the law, the worship, and the promises; to them belong the patriarchs, and from them, according to the flesh, comes the Messiah, who is over all, God blessed forever. Amen" (Rom 9:4–5).

CHRIST

FULFILLED AND CONFIRMED: JESUS AND THE TETRAGRAMMATON

> *Whoever has the word of Jesus for a true*
> *possession can also hear his silence.*
>
> —Ignatius of Antioch, *Ephesians* 15:2

CHRISTIANS HAVE TRADITIONALLY interpreted the Christian validity of such distinctively Jewish practices as circumcision and dietary laws according to the pattern of promise, fulfillment, and cancelation. According to this view, Christ fulfilled the promise inherent in such practices while making the practices themselves obsolete.[1] The interpretive pattern originated as a way of understanding Christ's reconciling death in relation to temple sacrifice (cf. Heb 9), but over time, Christians extended its application to the whole of the "ceremonial law"—that is, everything not concerned with morals or civil affairs. According to Thomas Aquinas, Christ's death fulfills and cancels every aspect of the ceremonial law, including dietary laws and circumcision.[2] Thomas held that it was a mortal sin for anyone to continue to observe such distinctively Jewish practices because it implied that the law's promise had not been fulfilled and that the Messiah had not come. An upshot of the teaching in its generalized form (which can be called economic supersessionism) is that insofar as Jews receive the gospel, they must cease to live as Jews, while insofar as they do not receive the gospel, their continued observance of Torah makes them odious to

God. In brief, the teaching suggests that God wanted Mary to be the last Jewish mother and Jesus to be the last Jew.[3]

Now, consider this hypothetical scenario. Suppose that Christians should discover one day that for the past two millennia, they had been practicing a part of Jewish ceremonial law without being aware of it. Suppose, moreover, the practice in question had been most salient in their conduct of worship—when reading Scripture, offering prayer, celebrating the sacraments, and so forth. What then should they do? Should they seek to uproot the practice from their worship as quickly and thoroughly as possible, on the grounds that Christ had canceled all such practices and made their continued observance sinful? Or should they take their cue from the liturgical rule *lex orandi est lex credendi et vivendi* (the rule of praying is the rule of believing and living) and conclude that since they themselves had been practicing the ceremonial law, Christ's fulfillment of it must not have rendered it comprehensively obsolete after all?

I will return to this question later. For now, I want to propose that something like this hypothetical scenario is in fact the case. The practice that I have in mind is that of avoiding the pronunciation of the Tetragrammaton, an ancient Jewish practice that serves as a token of reverence for the God who bears the Tetragrammaton and for the name itself. Knowingly or not, Christians have consistently hewed closely to this ancient bit of Jewish ceremonial law, especially in the conduct of their worship, and they have done so for a single simple reason. They have worshipped God following the precedent of the writers of the New Testament and above all of Jesus Christ himself, who observed the practice with unwavering scrupulosity.

Jesus's Name Avoidance in the Gospels

Most historians believe that the Jewish practice of avoiding the pronunciation of the Tetragrammaton was already centuries old by the beginning of the Common Era.[4] The precise motivations that gave birth to it are unknown, but pressure from certain biblical texts must certainly have played a role. While the third commandment's prohibition (Exod 20:7) was not limited to illicit speech acts involving the name, they were certainly within its scope and are the explicit theme of texts such as Deuteronomy 5:11 and Leviticus 24:11. In the latter passage, all those who were within earshot of a person who blasphemes the name are instructed to lay their hands on the perpetrator's head before stoning him, as though to cleanse themselves of having heard the blasphemy and return the contagion to its source. Texts such as these reflect the belief that verbal misuse of God's name is both sinful and dangerous for individuals and communities. Avoidance of the Divine Name, it seems, arose gradually in response to this generally felt circumstance. To use the terminology of later Jewish tradition, name avoidance reflects a form of building a fence around the law. Verbal misuse of the Tetragrammaton is avoided by avoiding its pronunciation altogether.[5]

What is certain is that by the beginning of the Common Era, Jews of every description assumed name avoidance to be obligatory. The Qumran sectarians prescribed banishment for those who pronounced the Name, even as more general titles for the Deity remained in circulation; the high priest in Jerusalem reserved its audible pronunciation for the most solemn of occasions; and even that jaded soldier and Jewish defector Josephus writes that he was forbidden to so much as speak of the name to outsiders.

Still, the most extensive body of evidence for the practice of name avoidance among Second Temple Jews is the collection of documents gathered in the New Testament of the Christian church. Early in the last century, a German doctoral student named Julius Boehmer noticed this fact and wrote a dissertation on the topic. "The New Testament," he wrote with some consternation, "is practically saturated with Jewish reticence before the name of God (*jüdische Scheu vor dem Namen Gottes*) . . . without exegetes to date having noticed."[6] He set about cataloging and categorizing all the figures of speech in the New Testament that bear the imprint of "Jewish reticence before the name of God" and arrived at a grand total of well over one thousand words and phrases. This is an astonishing number. In comparison, "Father" occurs as a designation for God a mere 260 times in the New Testament. If Boehmer's estimate is roughly correct, it means that chapter for chapter, the New Testament alludes to the Tetragrammaton about as often as does the Old, albeit in an apophatic manner that, as Boehmer correctly observed, is distinctively Jewish.

What Boehmer did not note is that the intensity of the New Testament's "reticence before the name of God" increases the closer one draws to the reported speech of the Jew Jesus of Nazareth.[7] It is not just that Jesus acquiesced to prevailing custom for form's sake. Rather, the Gospels indicate that he practiced and advocated a reserve toward the Divine Name that went beyond the conventions of the time. Jesus, it seems, was *hyperscrupulous* in his "reticence before the name of God."

This is evident in Jesus's furious rejection of oaths. Jesus's target was the idea that oaths became less binding in proportion to how indirectly they invoked God's name and person: the less direct the invocation, the less binding the oath. This view treats circumlocutions for the Divine Name as a kind of buffer that conveniently distances the speaker from the holiness of God, like the insulation of an electric wire. The more oblique the circumlocution, the less the majesty of God and God's name is implicated. Jesus will have nothing of it:

> Woe to you, blind guides, who say, "Whoever swears by the sanctuary is bound by nothing, but whoever swears by the gold of the sanctuary is bound by the oath." You blind fools! For which is greater, the gold or the sanctuary that has made the gold sacred? And you say, "Whoever swears by the altar is bound by nothing, but whoever swears by the gift that is on the altar is bound by the oath." How blind you are! For which is greater, the gift or the altar that makes the gift sacred? So whoever swears by the altar, swears by it and by everything on it; and whoever swears by the sanctuary, swears by it and by

the one who dwells in it; and whoever swears by heaven, swears by the throne of God and by the one who is seated upon it. (Matt 23:16–22)

Note that Jesus does not condemn the use of buffers in place of God's name. As Gustav Dalman observed about this passage over a century ago, "Even [Jesus] appears to approve the non-pronunciation of the name of God." Rather, Jesus's scorn is directed at the premise that circumlocutions *replace* the Divine Name rather than *refer* to it and its bearer. In Dalman's words, "Swearing by heaven is looked upon by Jesus as equivalent to swearing by God's name because *a real name of God was being intentionally avoided.*"[8] Here, as elsewhere, Jesus calls his disciples to a higher righteousness. That does not mean explicitly pronouncing the Tetragrammaton, as would be the case if Jesus regarded "reticence before the name of God" as an unworthy superstition or time-bound custom. Rather, Jesus advocates a yet more rigorous form of name avoidance: the eschewing of oaths altogether (Matt 5:33–36).

Dalman suggests that Jesus's teaching on oaths is connected to another feature of his speech—namely, his habit of emphasizing his teaching by introducing it with the word "amen" or even "amen amen." English translations almost always hide this extremely odd locution by rendering it as "truly" or "very truly." Yet the saying is deeply characteristic of Jesus's idiolect. The Synoptics report it some fifty times, and John twenty-five times:

"*Amen* I tell you, whoever does not receive the kingdom of God as a little child will never enter it." (Mark 10:15)[9]

"*Amen amen*, tell you, no one can see the kingdom of God without being born from above." (John 3:3)[10]

This use of "amen" is completely unattested in ancient literature outside the Gospels, and the Gospels themselves report it only of Jesus. What's going on? Dalman suggests that once again, "one may speak of a conscious avoidance of the name of God." Lacking recourse to the use of oaths, Jesus "had to seek for some other mode of emphasis, and found it in the solemner 'Amen.'"[11]

Yet another expression of Jesus's reserve toward the Divine Name is his custom of formulating his teaching in the passive voice, which makes the *patient* of some action the grammatical subject of the sentence while leaving the logical subject of the action unspecified. Joachim Jeremias dubbed the phenomenon the "divine passive" (*passivum divinum*) and estimated that it occurs some one hundred times in Jesus's speech as reported by the Gospels.[12] Indeed, the divine passive is so typical of Jesus that a full survey would amount to a recapitulation of his public ministry:

"Blessed are those who mourn, for they *will be comforted.*"
  (Matt 5:4)
"Blessed are the merciful, for they *will receive* mercy."
  (Matt 5:7)
"Blessed are the peacemakers, for they *will be called children
  of God.*" (Matt 5:9)
"Do not judge, so that you may *not be judged.*" (Matt 7:1)
"The heirs of the kingdom *will be thrown* into the outer
  darkness." (Matt 8:12)
"But the one who endures to the end *will be saved.*" (Matt
  24:13)
"Do not judge, and you will not *be judged*; do not condemn,
  and you will not *be condemned.* Forgive, and you will *be
  forgiven.*" (Luke 6:37)
"On that night there will be two in one bed; one *will be taken*
  and the other left." (Luke 17:34)
"All who exalt themselves *will be humbled,* but all who
  humble themselves *will be exalted.*" (Luke 18:14)
"I must proclaim the good news of the kingdom of God to
  the other cities also; for I *was sent* for this purpose." (Luke
  4:43)

"But after *I am raised up*, I will go ahead of you to Galilee."
   (Matt 26:32)
"All authority in heaven and on earth *has been given* to me."
   (Matt 28:18)

Yet granted its ubiquity in the Gospels, what does the divine passive have to do with Jesus's reserve toward God's name? The answer is clear. Like eschewing oaths and employing "amen" as a rhetorical intensifier, Jesus's habitual use of the passive voice gestures silently toward the Primordial Bearer of the Divine Name as the logical subject of his teaching while obviating the need to explicitly mention that bearer in any way at all.

The fact is that *jüdische Scheu vor dem Namen Gottes* colors virtually everything that Jesus says. The practice shapes and textures all his characteristic forms of speech, including his address to God as "Father" (Jesus couldn't address God using the Divine Name) and his teaching about the coming kingdom in "godless" parables (they leave God out of the picture entirely, like the divine passive). Nevertheless, Jesus's practice of not pronouncing God's name is not the cardinal concern of his ministry. It is only the outer token thereof. The cardinal concern itself is Jesus's zeal for the eschatological glorification of God's name. This is evident from the first petition of the Lord's Prayer: "Hallowed be your name!"

To hallow or sanctify the name of God is to vindicate its holiness, to remove from it every besmirching obscurity, and to make it shine forth with the radiance of a single truth only: "I am the LORD your God!" By placing this petition at the head of the prayer he taught to his disciples, Jesus indicates that every good thing they can hope for flows from this source.[13] Of course, the phrase "your name" refers to God's honor and reputation, the cloud of connotation that surrounds God's name. This cloud must become radiantly glorious if the petition is to be fulfilled. But the phrase *also* refers quite specifically to the Tetragrammaton itself, which Jesus leaves unspoken as a token of his reverence for it and its bearer.

Jesus's name reticence is not an incidental feature of the first petition but a clue to its meaning. It helps us understand Jesus's use of the passive voice: "Hallowed *be* your name!"[14] From a purely grammatical point of view, the passive voice always creates ambiguity because the logical subject of the verb is left unspecified. This ambiguity is evident in the variety of proposals Christians have made regarding *who* it is that is here called upon to hallow God's name, such as the church, creation, and so on. Once Jesus's customary practice of name avoidance is taken into account, however, the ambiguity disappears. The first petition is an appeal to *God's own zeal* on behalf of God's name. This zeal is attested throughout the Old Testament and is especially apparent in passages such as this from Ezekiel: "Thus says the Lord God: It is not for your sake, O house of Israel, that I am about to act, but for the sake of my holy name, which you have profaned among the nations to which you came. I will sanctify my great name, which has been profaned among the nations, and which you have profaned among them; and the nations shall know that I am the Lord, says the Lord God, when through you I display my holiness before their eyes" (Ezek 36:22–23).

The first petition of the Lord's Prayer is a human counterpart to Ezekiel 36, spoken with eschatological urgency. The sanctification of the Divine Name by anyone besides God does not come into question because all others (i.e., Israel and the nations) are the agents of its profanation in the first place. The only one who can sanctify the Divine Name is the Lord, its Primordial Bearer. Only the Lord can purify the cloud of connotation that surrounds it and make it shine forth with the radiant mystery that comes only from within. This will surely mean the redemption of Israel and the enlightenment of the nations (cf. Luke 2:32; Rom 15:9–12). Still, the first petition does not bid God to act for the sake of Israel or the nations. It bids God to act in fidelity to who God is for God's own name's sake.

In sum, Jesus's "reticence before the name of God," while consistent with the practice of Second Temple Judaism, has a distinctive theological significance of its own. Jesus's hyperscrupulous practice of name avoidance is the outer token of his messianic zeal for the end-time glorification of God's name. The practice renders a verdict on human God-talk that bids our vacuous and self-serving invocations of God's name to cease. It confesses our human inability to bear God's name in a way that corresponds to the glory of its eternal bearer. It divests itself of the Divine Name in hopeful longing that God will sanctify it at last as only God can do.

Jesus the Revealer of the Divine Name

But now, let us shift our attention to another aspect of the New Testament's witness to Jesus and the unspoken Tetragrammaton. Scholars such as Richard Bauckham, Larry Hurtado, and Joshua Coutts have shown that the New Testament writers portray the end-time glorification of the Divine Name for which Jesus prays as an event that has already begun and, indeed, as an event that coincides with the history that unfolds between Jesus and the One to whom he prays. Even as Jesus enforces reserve before the Divine Name with unsurpassed severity, *he is the site of its saving revelation to others* (cf. Phil 2:9–11).

As usual, the Fourth Gospel makes the point in its own extraordinary idiom. John makes no report of a prayer that Jesus teaches to his disciples. Instead, we find near the middle of the Gospel a prayer that Jesus himself prays which consists in a single petition: "Father, glorify your name" (John 12:28). The centrality of this prayer to the design of the Fourth Gospel is confirmed by the fact that it provides the only occasion when the Gospel reports the Father's own direct discourse. The Father replies to Jesus's prayer by saying, "I have glorified it, and I will glorify it again" (John 12:28).

This exchange is the only "conversation" between God and Jesus that the New Testament reports; strikingly, its topic is God's name, the Tetragrammaton.[15] The evangelist signals reticence before the Primordial Bearer of the Divine Name by identifying the transcendent speaker as a "voice from heaven" rather than as "God" or as "Father." With words that are audible to Jesus but that sound like thunder to the crowd, the "voice from above" reveals the divine purpose for the sake of which Jesus was sent: the glorification of the Divine Name. A few chapters later, at the very end of the High Priestly Prayer, Jesus tells the Father that he is about to accomplish his mission using words that exactly mirror the Father's words to him: "I made your name known to them, and I will make it known, so that the love with which you have loved me may be in them, and I in them" (John 17:26). With this saying, the "conversation" between Jesus and the "voice from above" ends; the Gospel reports no further words exchanged between them.

In the High Priestly Prayer itself, Jesus casts light on how it is possible for him to fulfill his mission. He himself is the bearer of "your name *that you have given me*" (John 17:11, 12; italics added). The Fourth Gospel invites the reader to understand that Jesus bears the Divine Name not only in time but also in eternity. It does so by sprinkling Jesus's "I am" statements through the Gospel like breadcrumbs through a forest. Among these is the saying "Before Abraham was, I am" (John 8:58). Jesus repeats this name one last time when he is arrested by the soldiers on the eve of his crucifixion, thereby striking them to the ground and fulfilling the Lord's prophecy that "to me every knee shall bow" (John 18:4–8; cf. Isa 45:24). Once again, however, we must not lose sight of the fact that "I am" is not "the Divine Name that Jesus is said to have been given."[16] Distinct from the Tetragrammaton yet closely linked to it, the words "I am" permit Jesus to reveal his identity as the eternal receiver of the Divine Name while leaving the Name itself unspoken.

For our purposes, the point to underscore is this: Even when modulated into the highest pitch of christological fulfillment, the New Testament's witness to the glorification of the Divine Name preserves the form of *jüdische Scheu vor dem Namen Gottes*. Here the pattern of promise, fulfillment, and cancelation cannot describe what is going on. Instead, we must speak of a pattern of promise, fulfillment, and confirmation.

A Hypothetical Scenario Revisited

The practice of name avoidance was not only characteristic of Second Temple Judaism. It has also been characteristic of the two great religious traditions that stem from that period, Judaism and Christianity. But while Jews have avoided the pronunciation of the Tetragrammaton in full cognizance of what they are doing, Christians generally have not. A telling illustration of this appears in the following statement by the German theologian Otto Weber (1902–66): "Why then, we must ask, do [Christians] not say 'Yahweh'? The only possible answer is that the name Yahweh belongs to the old covenant. . . . It does not occur in the New Testament. . . . Just as Christ is the goal and thus the 'end' of the law, the name Yahweh attains its goal and its 'end' in him. . . . The name Yahweh belongs as a name to the unfulfilled law, to the promise, to the old covenant. . . . If the Church still wanted to say 'Yahweh' (or perhaps) 'Jehovah,' then it would be denying what God has done."[17]

For all its extravagant wrongheadedness, Weber's statement contains an unintended grain of truth. Whenever Christians have insisted on pronouncing the Tetragrammaton in the context of the church's worship, they have indeed deviated in an important way from the example of the New Testament. Contrary to what Weber supposes, however, the deviation consists not in assigning a sacred significance to the Divine Name that the New Testament does not. Rather, it consists in failing to recognize and honor the Tetragrammaton in the distinctively Jewish register that the New Testament employs—namely, reverent nonpronunciation.

Once Christians become aware of this fact, however, they are faced with the dilemma that we noted at the start of this chapter. Christians have traditionally interpreted distinctively Jewish practices such as circumcision and dietary laws according to the pattern of promise, fulfillment, and cancelation. Name avoidance is one such distinctively Jewish practice. Therefore, it seems that Christians should "cancel" name avoidance. And yet for nearly two millennia, they have not. It is true that Christians have not been as consistent about this as Jews have been. Since the medieval period, Christians have sometimes used vocalized forms of the Tetragrammaton in both academic and liturgical settings, and they still do so today when singing hymns such as "Guide Me O Thou Great Jehovah." Yet such cases amount to something like "the exception that proves the rule" when weighed against Christian history as a whole. Overwhelmingly, Christians have avoided pronouncing the Tetragrammaton, especially when reading the Scriptures, celebrating the sacraments, and so on. What then should they do?

One option that won't work is to invoke Augustine's theory that the validity of the Mosaic law is divided into *tria tempora* (three periods of time). The first period is the time before Christ, when the ceremonial laws were valid and preparatory of Christ, while the third period is the one that the contemporary church inhabits, when the gospel is widely proclaimed throughout the world and the continued observance of the Mosaic law is a sin. Augustine noticed that the apostles themselves did not fit into either of these times, since they lived after Christ's passion and resurrection and yet continued to observe the law, offer sacrifices in the temple, and so on (cf. Acts 15, 21). He therefore proposed the existence of a middle period that fell after Christ's resurrection but before the gospel had begun to be widely proclaimed. During this second period, Augustine maintained, the Mosaic law was "dead but not yet deadly," meaning its observance afforded no benefits but was not yet sinful. Augustine's theory is an ingenious way of making the interpretive pattern of promise, fulfillment, and cancelation seem to fit the data of the New Testament, but it clearly will not help in this case. The problem is that Christians did not cease the practice of name avoidance at the end of the second period but have continued to observe it to the present day.

Another option would be to double down on the pattern of promise, fulfillment, and cancelation. If the pattern conflicts with Christianity's historic practice of name avoidance, then so much the worse for name avoidance. This is the official stance of the Jehovah's

Witnesses, who maintain that the suppression of the Divine Name in Christian worship was a catastrophic surrender to Jewish superstition that adulterated the church almost from its inception. A similar conviction has spurred countless Christian translators of the Bible from the sixteenth century to the present to transliterate the Tetragrammaton whenever it appears in the Old Testament.[18] It was also the view of Julius Boehmer, the German biblical scholar who documented how pervasively name avoidance shaped the language of the New Testament. Boehmer hypothesized that the practice originated in Jewish cultic practices and, by the New Testament era, had overrun everyday life. "We are all under its influence, almost always unconsciously," Boehmer lamented, "and suffer from it in many ways." Boehmer hoped his study would make Christians more aware of the fact and spur them to counteract it.[19]

Yet however fervently its advocates embrace it, this option faces a huge obstacle: the New Testament. As Boehmer himself recognized, name avoidance saturates it from beginning to end. Short of jettisoning the New Testament from the church or subjecting it to massive redaction, name avoidance will remain at the heart of Christian worship for the simple reason that it is inextricable from the witness of New Testament writers and above all from the Gospels' portraits of Jesus Christ.

The final option is to conclude that the pattern of promise, fulfillment, and cancelation must not be *comprehensively* valid after all. Matthew Levering has defended the pattern of promise, fulfillment, and cancelation by arguing that "the Messiah of all peoples has come and has eschatologically re-ordered the Mosaic law around himself."[20] While I agree with Levering that the Messiah has come and eschatologically reordered the Mosaic law around himself, I do not think that it necessarily follows that this reordering always entails the law's obsolescence in the life of the church. In some cases, it does, as the writer of Hebrews affirms with respect to temple sacrifice. But the church's own practice of name avoidance shows that it is an error for Christians to generalize this to the ceremonial law as a whole. Here, as I've already stated, we must speak in terms of a pattern of promise, fulfillment, and *confirmation.*

In 2008, a similar conclusion was reached by the Vatican's Congregation for Divine Worship and the Discipline of the Sacraments. In an official document entitled *Letter to the Bishop's Conferences on "The Name of God,"* the Congregation expressly prohibited the use of vocalized forms of the Tetragrammaton in Roman Catholic worship, noting with disapproval that in recent years, the practice had "crept in . . . in the reading of biblical texts taken from the Lectionary as well as in prayers and hymns."[21] What is especially important about the Congregation's letter is the rationale that it provides for its prohibition. As we saw earlier, Otto Weber also rejected the vocalized Tetragrammaton in Christian worship, but he did so on the grounds that Christ's fulfillment of the Old Testament had rendered it a thing of the past. In contrast, the Congregation consistently refers to the Tetragrammaton in terms of the highest respect, calling it "the God of Israel's proper name," "the Divine Name," "the sacred tetragrammaton," and "the sacred name of God himself." The letter explains that the practice of using a surrogate in place of the name arose "prior to the Christian era" as an acknowledgment of its status as "an expression of the infinite greatness and majesty of God." The writers of the New Testament, in turn, adopted the practice with the same understanding, a fact that "has important implications for New Testament christology itself." After citing several passages from the New Testament substantiating this claim, the letter concludes by declaring that the church has "its own grounds" for not pronouncing the name of God.[22] It is a matter of remaining faithful to the church's own tradition, which, in this case, is the tradition of the Jewish people as well.

{ 6 }

CHURCH

PEOPLE OF GOD, BODY OF CHRIST, TEMPLE OF THE SPIRIT: AN ECOSYSTEM OF PRAISE

RECENT ECUMENICAL ECCLESIOLOGY has emphasized the church's rootedness in the Holy Trinity. An expression of this is the practice of organizing discussions of the church under three rubrics: "people of God," "body of Christ," and "temple of the Holy Spirit."[1] The headings commend themselves because they represent the variety of New Testament images for the church, but even more because they signal that the nature and mission of the church manifests a Trinitarian form. The headings indicate that the church is related to each of the persons of the Trinity in a special way that is different from the way in which it is joined to the other two persons. So, for example, the church is the body of Christ, and not the body of the Spirit or of the Father. At the same time, the three rubrics together remind us that the church's special relationship to any one person always involves understanding its relationship to all three, for "the works of the Trinity *ad extra* are undivided." This means that to understand the church as the body of Christ, it is necessary to understand it simultaneously as the people of God and the temple of the Spirit. The three ecclesial motifs refer not to three different things but to the same thing under three different aspects: the "one, holy, catholic, and apostolic church," whose life is a song of praise to the Holy Trinity, from whom, in whom, and through whom it lives.

One theologian who has used the triad of images to organize his ecclesiology is Robert W. Jenson. Jenson stands out among contemporary theologians for the boldness with which he brought

111

the doctrine of the Trinity to bear on a range of challenging topics, including that of understanding the church in a way that coheres with the church's own recent affirmation of God's irrevocable election of the Jewish people. In his *Systematic Theology*, Jenson develops his account of the church's relationship to the Jewish people under the rubric the "people of God," following the precedent of the Second Vatican Council's groundbreaking discussion of *De populo Dei* in *Lumen Gentium*, which affirms of the Jews that "on account of their fathers this people remains most dear to God, for God does not repent of the gifts He makes nor of the calls He issues."[2] Jenson's own rich discussion includes the following affirmations:

- "What is often labelled 'supersessionism' . . . must be and is being overcome: that is, the theologumenon . . . that the church succeeds Israel in such a fashion as to *displace* from the status of God's people those Jews who do not enter the church."
- "When the New Testament refers to the people of God it rarely has the church in mind. The nation of Israel continues to appear as 'the people' of God . . . and when the New Testament does refer to the church as God's people, this is . . . done at least in part to identify her with Israel."
- "The people whom, according to Paul, God has not rejected is Israel constituted as a people in her own ancient ways of national continuity, that is, by the unity of tribal descent with certain religious, legal, and civil intuitions, most notably effected by circumcision."
- "The church . . . should regard the continuing synagogue as a detour like herself, within the Fulfillment of Israel's hope."
- "The church *is* the people of God can be an exclusive proposition only eschatologically."[3]

These are all affirmations with which I generally agree, but the focus of this chapter is not Jenson's theology of Israel. The question I want to pursue is how we should understand this or a similar account of the church as the people of God in relation to the church's identity as the body of Christ and as the temple of the Spirit. A post- or nonsupersessionist account of the church as the people of God will be convincing only if it contributes to a compelling account of the church's rootedness in the life of the Trinity as a whole. As Jenson writes, "It must be the task of systematic theology to take 'The church is the people of God, the temple of the Spirit, and the body of Christ' with epistemic seriousness by displaying the conceptual links between these phrases."[4] That challenge is the focus of this chapter.

The Church as an Ecosystem of Praise

I want to begin my account of the church as the people of God, the body of Christ, and the temple of the Spirit by considering a passage from Irenaeus of Lyon. In *Apostolic Preaching*, Irenaeus proposes that the one God who made and fashioned all things relates to humankind in different ways: "To the faithful He is as Father, since 'in the last times' He opened the testament of the adoption as sons; while to the Jews He is as Lord and Lawgiver, since in the intervening period, when mankind had forgotten, abandoned and rebelled against God, He brought them into slavery by means of the Law, that they might learn that they have [as] Lord the Maker and Fashioner . . . ; and to the Gentiles He is as Creator and Almighty."[5]

According to Irenaeus, the one God relates to humankind in three different ways that are characterized by the special "name" or "face" that God presents to that portion of humanity. To "the faithful," God is "as Father"; to the Jews, as "Lord and Lawgiver"; and to the gentiles, "as Creator and Almighty."

A casual reading of the passage in isolation might suggest that Irenaeus thinks that God's different postures toward humanity result in three nonoverlapping experiences of God. If that were the case, then a person who came to know God "as Father" by entering the "covenant of adoption" would cease to know and experience God as they had formerly done as a Jew or as a gentile. Moreover, Jews and gentiles themselves would know God in ways that were unconnected to each other. However, a careful reading of the passage in context shows that this is not what Irenaeus thinks. Immediately prior to this passage, Irenaeus writes, "And the Father is called by the Spirit 'Most High' and 'Almighty' and 'Lord of Hosts' that we may learn [that] the God, this one Himself, He is the Maker of heaven and earth and the whole world, the Creator of angels and men, and the Lord of all, by whom all things exist, and from whom all things are nourished—merciful, compassionate, good, righteous, the God of all—both of the Jews and of the Gentiles and of the faithful."[6]

This passage makes clear that Irenaeus understands the Father's identity to include the "names" or "faces" that God presents to both Jews and gentiles. Irenaeus's opponent Marcion had understood the Father's self-revelation to be the announcement of a hitherto completely unknown God. In contrast, Irenaeus understands it to incorporate what Jews and gentiles already truly know about God based on God's goodness toward all. This knowledge includes belief in God as Creator, which is common to Jew and gentile, although in our first passage, Irenaeus used slightly different vocabularies to express the belief in each case. But it also includes the distinctive names that Scripture associates with God's "face" as made known to the Jews, such as "Most High" and "Lord of Hosts." (Like most patristic theologians, Irenaeus appears to have been ignorant of the Tetragrammaton, but he is alert to the special biblical resonance of its common surrogate "Lord.") In sum, Irenaeus and Marcion would likely agree that addressing God "as Father" is a distinguishing mark of the church, but they would disagree about the significance of the term itself. For Marcion, the very fatherhood of the Father, as it were, depends on the name's exclusion of characteristically Jewish and gentile beliefs about God, whereas for Irenaeus, the opposite is true. For Irenaeus, the fatherhood of the Father is displayed by the fact that he is with equal propriety the bearer of names that are already known and praised by Israel and the nations.

There is an elegant simplicity, I think, to Irenaeus's understanding of the church's relationship to Jews and gentiles. The church stands in critical solidarity with both groups, sharing their distinctive vantage points on God's names and goodness while also joining these together in light of its own. The church is a kind of ecosystem of praise, as it were, made up of different fields of doxology that overlap in the "covenant of adoption" while extending outward in ways that are shared by all humankind.

While my proposal lacks the elegance of Irenaeus, I do intend it to be similarly simple, at least in its basic outline. I propose that when we describe the church as the people of God, the body of Christ, and the temple of the Spirit, we illuminate from different angles its character as an "ecosystem of praise" rooted in the life of the Trinity whose persons bear a panoply of Divine Name(s) in characteristically different ways:

- As the people of God, the church is united in a special way to the first person of the Trinity, the Primordial Bearer of the unspoken Tetragrammaton. Viewed from this perspective, the church's ecosystem of praise is shaped by its critical solidarity with the Jewish people, the people whom God has irrevocably elected for the purpose of living to the glory of the Father's name. With Israel, the church confesses "Hear O Israel, the LORD our God, the LORD is one" (Deut 6:4 TLV), even as it also confesses "For us there is one God, the Father . . . and one Lord Jesus Christ" (1 Cor 8:6). A humanly unbridgeable chasm separates normative Judaism from the church's confession of Jesus as the primordial receiver of the Father's name (John 17:11–12). Despite this chasm, the church lives in confidence that the Lord's fidelity to the Divine Name will ultimately redound to the salvation of "all Israel" (Rom 11:26).

- As the temple of the Holy Spirit, the church is united in a special way to the third person of the Trinity, the person whose unique hypostatic identity is signified by common nouns. Viewed from this perspective, the church's ecosystem of praise is shaped by its critical solidarity with all the communities of the earth, and especially with those whose members have already entered the church. In common with these communities, the church praises God using common nouns drawn from the sacred and secular life of all peoples, tribes, and nations, even as it repurposes those common nouns for praise of the Trinity. As a gathering of the nations in the midst of the nations, the church seeks to fulfill its commission to preach the gospel in such a way that at last, all peoples may confess, "In our own languages we hear them speaking about God's deeds of power" (Acts 2:11).

- As the body of Christ, the church is united in a special way to the second person of the Trinity, identified by the church's liturgy of baptism as "the Son" (Matt 28:19). Viewed from this perspective, the church's ecosystem of praise is shaped by its union with Jesus Christ the Son of God, who is the head of his body, the church (Col 1:18). As the Word made flesh, Christ's own characteristic speech to the one God is itself an "ecosystem of praise," which affords a place not only to the vocabulary of divine kinship but also to God's proper name and to common nouns ("Our Father, hallowed be your name, your kingdom come!"). Just so, baptism into Christ shapes the church as a body with many members, both Jew and gentile (1 Cor 12:12–13). What makes Christ's body a luminous sign of the new creation is that it incorporates Jew and gentile into Christ's filial address to God as "Father" in such a way that their distinctive modes of praise are united but not destroyed (Luke 2:32; Rom 15:9–12).

The rest of this chapter develops this outline in greater detail. The way it does so, however, calls for a final word of introduction. The Western church's understanding of the church's rootedness in the Trinity has been shaped to a great extent by Augustine of Hippo, and in particular, by his analysis of the Father's sending of the Son and Spirit in the "fullness of time" (Gal 4:4). Because of Augustine's outsized influence, I develop my proposal in running conversation with him. Granted, this risks overburdening the chapter beyond rescue. Still, my hope is that Augustine will help me vividly display the "conceptual links" that connect our three ecclesial images and show how together they support a postsupersessionist account of the church.

The Church as People of God: Solidarity with Israel in Praise of the Lord

All the peoples of the earth shall see that you are
called by the name of the Lord. (Deut 28:10)

Since Augustine, it has been a commonplace of Western theology to say that only the Son and the Holy Spirit have missions. The Father has no mission because he is not sent. What the tradition then sometimes omits to note, however, is that the "missionless" Father does have a *purpose* for the sake of which he sends the Son and Spirit into the world. We can and should describe that purpose as the rescue of fallen humanity from sin and death. But to describe the Father's purpose solely as a rescue mission is to call a halt in the upland meadows of the biblical witness, as it were. We ascend a good stretch higher if we affirm, with Augustine, that the purpose of the Father's sending of the Son and Spirit in time is to reveal their origins in eternity. The Son's mission in time reveals his eternal generation from the Father, just as the Spirit's mission reveals its eternal procession from the Father and the Son. But even this stops short of the Bible's loftiest peaks as Augustine spies them. For the revelation of the eternal processions of the Son and Spirit stands in service of the revelation of the eternal identity of the Father, the Unoriginate Origin of the divine life, knowledge of whom constitutes the eternal beatitude of creatures. The Second Vatican Council's decree *Ad gentes* makes this point beautifully when it states, "And so at last, there will be realized the plan of our Creator, who formed man to His own image and likeness, when all who share one human nature, regenerated in Christ through the Holy Spirit and beholding the glory of God, will be able to say with one accord: 'Our Father.'"[7]

When we understand the Father's purpose in this way, we see salvation history, apprehended in its "most general proportion" (Jonathan Edwards), as a majestic unity that runs *a Patri ad Patrem*, from the Father as the Unoriginate Origin of the divine life to the Father as the final goal of creaturely doxology.[8]

I find this a compelling account of the Bible's theological unity at the largest scale. Nevertheless, I have a bone to pick with it. Precisely when we try to describe salvation history in its "most general proportion," we are led astray by a monochromatic use of the kinship vocabulary of "Father, Son, and Spirit." According to the relentless testimony of the Old Testament and the New, it is simply not possible to say *who* the Father is apart from the Father's *name*. And the Father's name is not "Father." It is the Tetragrammaton. It is in view of this name that the Scriptures ubiquitously name and praise the first person as the Lord, or, in the periphrastic speech of the New Testament, as "[he] who is and who was and who is to come" (Rev 1:4), "the Blessed" (Mark 14:61), "the Power" (Mark 14:62), "the Majestic Glory" (2 Pet 1:17), and so on. *Ad gentes* would have made its point with even greater scriptural cogency if it had concluded with the words "Our Father, *hallowed be your Name!*"

To be sure, we do not name the first person more truly as "the Blessed" than as "Father." It is not as though the Unoriginate Origin were first primordially the "Lord" and then only subsequently the "one God and Father" (Eph 4:6). Rather, it is a question of logical priority among equally appropriate names that must ultimately be understood in light of one another. Kornelis Miskotte was correct when he wrote, "Father is more truly an epithet of the Name than the reverse, according to which the Name and its root, YHWH, would be an epithet or clarifying addendum to the name Father which we already know."[9] We signify the primordiality of the Father's hypostatic identity more distinctly when we identify him as the Unoriginate Bearer and Giver of the unspoken Tetragrammaton than when we employ the analogical term "Father." Just as it is impossible to go behind the first person to some more basic ontological reality, so it is impossible to go behind the Tetra-grammaton to some more basic lexical sign. To the extent that the "target" of salvation history is knowledge of the first person in the ineffable uniqueness of its hypostatic identity, we must say that the paternal purpose that encompasses salvation history is the glorification of God the Father as the Primordial Bearer of the unspoken Tetragrammaton. Formulated with complete strictness, therefore, we should say that the course of salvation history runs from *Alpha* to *Omega*, where each word singly and both together are to be understood as surrogates for the first person of the Trinity, the Primordial Bearer and Giver of the Divine Name, the One iden-tified by John of Patmos in aberrant Greek as "He who is and who was and who is coming" (Rev 1:8).[10]

This refinement of our perception of salvation history in its most general proportion has cascading effects that shape our understanding of the canon of Scripture at ever-closer ranges, down to the finest detail. When we understand salvation history as running *a Patri ad Patrem* in absence of the Divine Name, it is all too easy to pass quickly through the Old Testament on the way to the New. The Old Testament "people of God" becomes an amorphous, vaporous quantity that lacks defining features and a proper name of its own. In contrast, when we understand salvation history as running from *Alpha* to *Omega*, we keep bumping into a sharp-edged and deeply mysterious fact: the Creator of all things has chosen to forever bind his proper name with the proper name of a particular people, the Jews.

Karl Barth was sensitive to the issue I am pressing. He attempted to do justice to God's election of Israel by making it inter-nal to God's eternal election of grace in Jesus Christ, and by making God's election of grace internal to the doctrine of God. So far so good. The problem is Barth's conception of the *purpose* for the sake of which God elects Israel, which he specified as that of witnessing to God's verdict of No! against sinful humanity, a judgment that God brings to completion with Jesus's death on the cross. Barth's first move opened a path for Christians to envision the unity of the Bible in a way that is both christocentric and postsupersessionist. Barth's second move prohibited Barth himself from traveling far down that path.[11]

With Barth, we should affirm that God's eternal decree of grace in Jesus Christ is the foundation of God's election of Israel. Contra Barth, however, we should affirm that within this decree, God elects Israel for the special purpose of living to the glory of the Father as the bearer of his name, the Tetragrammaton. That is why God's covenant with Israel comes with no "expiration date." For unlike God's no, the Father's identity as the Primordial Bearer of this name is never-ending (cf. Exod 3:15). To be sure, the goal of salvation history is "larger" than Israel. It is the endless morning when Israel and the nations and all creation will sing back and forth "The LORD is God" in praise of the Father's glory. But it has pleased the Majestic Glory that there be a people set apart by name for the purpose of glorifying the Divine Name in a unique way: by living root and branch from the LORD's faithfulness to it (Ezek 36:22).

This account has important implications for our understanding of the church as "the people of God." The moniker identifies the church in terms of the special way it is united to the first person of the Trinity, and so also to the ultimate "paterological" goal of salvation history: the glorification of the Father's name (John 12:28; Rom 15:9). But it is the Jewish people whom the Father set apart for the sake of this purpose, originally (Rom 9:1–5) and irrevocably (Rom 11:29), just as it is the Jewish people that has chiefly borne the costs of this purpose through the ages. The church can therefore be "the people of God" only insofar as it participates in God's unfinished history of covenant faithfulness with the whole Jewish people, irrespective of its posture toward the gospel (cf. Rom 9–11). The prayer that John Paul II slipped into a crevice in the western wall of the temple in Jerusalem reflects a similar understanding: "God of our fathers, you chose Abraham and his descendants to bring your name to the nations. We are deeply saddened by the behavior of those who in the course of history have caused these children of yours to suffer. And asking your forgiveness, we wish to commit ourselves to genuine brotherhood with the people of the covenant."[12]

The church is the eschatologically enlarged people of God, reshaped around the Father's sending of the Son and Spirit in "the fullness of time" (Gal 4:4). But just as the missions of the Son and Spirit serve the glorification of the Father's name, so the church can be the enlarged people of God only together with the Jews or not at all (cf. Rom 11:18).

In the second place, this understanding of Israel's vocation clarifies why the ecclesial people of God exists perpetually as a community of Jews and gentiles (cf. Acts 15) and not just as the ingathering of all the children of Adam. The Roman Catholic document "The Gifts and the Calling of God Are Irrevocable" (2015) expresses a profound truth when it states, "It is and remains a qualitative definition of the Church of the New Covenant that it consists of Jews and Gentiles, even if the quantitative proportions of Jewish and Gentile Christians may initially give a different impression."[13] Karl Barth was on the right track when he proposed that the church exhibits an internal "differentiation" between Jew and gentile that "confirms its unity" and serves as the enduring sign of its identity as the people God.[14] But again, Barth's reach is too short when he assigns to Jewish followers of Jesus the role of witnessing to God's severity and to gentiles that of witnessing to God's mercy. The deepest foundation of the church as an ecosystem of praise gathered from Israel and the nations is the plenitude of the Father's name(s). As the canon attests from beginning to end, the Father is "the LORD God" (Gen 2:4; cf. Luke 1:32; Rev 1:8). Israel's special vocation is to glorify the Father precisely insofar as he is the Primordial Bearer of the Divine Name, the Tetragrammaton. From the Christian perspective, baptism "eschatologically re-orders" (Levering) this vocation around Jesus Christ, the eternal receiver of the Father's unspoken name (cf. John 17:11, 12).[15] But in this way, baptism *confirms* rather than *cancels* Israel's primordial vocation. Because baptism confirms Jews in their vocation to praise the Father's name, they remain constitutionally best suited to lead the whole church in offering praise to the Father in the name of Jesus that takes the form "the Lᴏʀᴅ is God!" (cf. Rom 15:9). Here the *ecclesia ex gentibus* properly allows the *ecclesia ex circumcisione* to take the lead in the "call and response" that characterizes the "differentiated unity" of the church's life of praise.[16]

At the same time, of course, there is a closely related form of praise that the *ecclesia ex gentibus* is constitutionally best suited to lead. This brings us to a consideration of the church as the temple of the Holy Spirit.

The Church as the Temple of the Spirit: Solidarity with the Nations in Praise of "Our God"

From one ancestor he made all nations to inhabit the whole earth, and he allotted the times of their existence and the boundaries of the places where they would live, so that they would search for God and perhaps grope for him and find him—though indeed he is not far from each one of us. For "In him we live and move and have our being"; as even some of your own poets have said, "For we too are his offspring." (Acts 17:26–28)

One of Augustine's advances over earlier generations of "economic Trinitarians" such as Irenaeus is sometimes said to be his emphatic articulation of the unprecedented novelty of the incarnation.[17] The "economic" theologians who wrote prior to Augustine found plentiful "christophanies" in the Old Testament that anticipated the incarnation and formed sinews of continuity between the Testaments. In contrast, Augustine's reading of the canon pivots on the claim that the Father does not "send" the Son prior to "the fullness of time" (Gal 4:4; cf. *Trinity*, bk. 4). The sending of the Son is identical with the incarnation, and it is the incarnation that first reveals the Son's eternal generation from the Father. This means that, for Augustine, the Father too is not revealed before "the fullness of time." For since the Father lacks a visible mission of his own, he is dependent on the Son and Spirit to make him known. From this vantage point, Augustine vigorously dismantles centuries of earlier exegesis that had emphasized the unity of the Testaments by discerning anticipatory appearances of the persons of the Trinity in the Old Testament.[18]

While it is no doubt important for Christian theology to convincingly depict the novelty of the incarnation, Augustine here gives us too much of a good thing. At the extreme, Augustine's reading tends to bifurcate the canon by overweighting the New Testament and evacuating the Old of Trinitarian significance. In my opinion, however, the problem lies not with Augustine's insistence on the novelty of the incarnation as such. There I believe he is on solid ground, as I will later explain. Rather, the miscue is Augustine's seemingly innocuous claim that the Father has no visible mission. To be sure, the claim is strictly true, for, indeed, the Father is neither *visible* nor *sent.* Nevertheless, the claim easily misleads by causing us to overlook a point on which Robert Jenson vigorously and rightly insists. While the Father has no visible mission, he does have a distinctive mode of spatiotemporal manifestation: the Father *speaks.* By means of audible speech, the Father reveals his unique hypostatic identity as the Primordial Bearer of the Divine Name and as the Unoriginate Origin of all things eternal and temporal. Moreover, as the New Testament itself insists, the Father's self-identifying speech originates in the *Old* Testament, not in the New. The Letter to the Hebrews makes the point with perfect clarity: "Long ago God spoke to our ancestors in many and various ways by the prophets, but in these last days he has spoken to us by a Son" (Heb 1:1–2). To be sure, the Father speaks in *a new way* when he speaks "by a Son." The Father's speech is "eschatologically reordered" (Levering) around the person of Jesus (John 12:28). But the fact remains that the Father's audible speech provides an arc of continuity—indeed, *the* arc of continuity—that unites the Testaments. In the words of Irenaeus of Lyon, "There is one and the same Father, whose voice from the beginning even to the end is present with His handiwork."[19] When Christian theology forgets not only the Father's *name* but also the Father's audible *voice*, the canon's spine is all but broken.[20]

Happily, when we turn from Augustine's account of the spatiotemporal manifestation of the Father to that of the Holy Spirit, we get more helpful guidance. Here Augustine makes just the move that I wish he had made with respect to the voice of the Father. Augustine holds that the Spirit's visible mission in "the fullness of time" manifests a *relative* rather than *absolute* novelty relative to the Old Testament:

> As for what the evangelist says, if the Spirit was not yet given because Jesus was not yet glorified (John 7:39), how are we to understand it, except as saying that there was going to be a kind of giving or sending such as there had never been before? It is not that there had been none before, but rather none of this kind. If the Holy Spirit had not been given at all before, what were the prophets filled with when they spoke?[21]

Augustine here clearly implies that the Spirit was already personally active in Old Testament prophecy, even if not in the same way as in the New. He then immediately goes on to put his finger on a vital stream of Spirit-filled novelty-in-continuity that forms a sinew of continuity between the Testaments. This sinew concerns what we might call the *doxological destiny* of the world's languages—that is, their foreordination for the proclamation and hearing of the gospel, and so for the eschatological glorification of the triune God:

> Nowhere else do we read that men had spoken languages they did not know as the Holy Spirit came upon them, in the way that occurred at Pentecost. For then his coming needed to be demonstrated by perceptible signs, to show that the whole world and all nations with their variety of languages were going to believe in Christ by the gift of the Holy Spirit, in order to fulfill the psalmist's prophetic song, *There are no languages or dialects whose voices are not*

*heard; their sound has gone out to all the earth, and their words
to the end of the world* (Ps 19:3).[22]

Note that while the Spirit actualized the "doxological destiny"
of the world's languages in a new way on the morning of Pentecost,
the Spirit was already at work in the Old Testament anticipating
this event in the prophetic words of Psalm 19. And not only there!
Augustine's citation of Psalm 19 directs our attention to a broad
seam of biblical witness in which the Christian imagination dis-
cerns, in the light *of* Pentecost, signs of God's providential order-
ing of the life of the nations in preparation *for* Pentecost. The early
church sometimes spoke of this as a *praeparatio evangelica,* meaning God's advance work among cultures preparing them to receive
the gospel, but I think we might speak even more aptly of this work
as a preparation of the day of Pentecost. This preparation is inaugurated prior to the fall in God's blessing "Be fruitful and multiply,
and fill the earth" (Gen 1:28) and is reaffirmed in the postlapsarian
world in the Table of Nations (Gen 10) and the story of Babel (Gen
11). Viewed from this "gentile-centric" perspective, even God's
calling of Abraham concerns the blessing of the nations (Gen 12:3;
cf. Isa 19:24–25). Paul's sermon to the Athenians, quoted at the head
of this section, places the whole of salvation history from Adam
to Christ in a light that foregrounds God's saving work among the
gentiles, to the point where Israel as the *people* of God disappears
into the larger history of God's generous and evenhanded—if also
hidden and mysterious—providence among the *peoples* of God.
From this vantage point, we would have to be shocked if the last
book of the Christian canon did not contain verses relating visions
such as this: "a great multitude that no one could count, from every
nation, from all tribes and peoples and languages. . . . saying, 'Salvation belongs to *our God* [!] who is seated on the throne, and to the
Lamb!'" (Rev 7:9–10; italics added).

An important theme of the Christian canon read in a "gentile-
forward" way is that of the eschatological temple of God. For the
purposes in this chapter, the crucial thing to observe is that it is

precisely the presence of *gentiles* that marks out God's temple as *eschatological.* This theme, already crystal clear in the Old Testament (Ps 96:7–8; Isa 2:2–3; 25:6; 56:6–7; 66:23; Jer 3:17; Mic 4:1–2; Zech 14:16), is crucial for understanding New Testament allusions to the church as temple. At the Council of Jerusalem (Acts 15), James provides the clinching rationale for admitting gentiles *as gentiles* into the fellowship of Jesus by recalling a prophecy that the rebuilt temple ("the dwelling of David") will be open to "all other peoples . . . even all the Gentiles" (Acts 15:17).[23] We find the same association of ideas in Ephesians 2:11–22 and 1 Peter 2:4–10, both key passages for the theme of the church as the temple of God, built up in the power of the Spirit.

Surely, if the presence of gentiles *as* gentiles is the sine qua non of the church as the Spirit-enlivened eschatological temple of God, then they cannot be without some distinctive contribution to the church's sacrifice of praise and thanksgiving. In the previous section, I proposed that we discern the deepest foundation of Israel's election in its vocation to glorify the Primordial Bearer of the Divine Name. Now I wish to propose something similar with respect to the gentiles gathered into the church from all the peoples under heaven. Gentiles adorn the eschatological temple of God with praise as only they can do—by offering up the riches of language, culture, and conception that the Spirit has prepared beforehand in the lives of all peoples, tribes, and nations. If Israel's vocation comes to fruition when it calls out to the nations, "*The* LORD is God," the Spirit's hidden work among the nations bears fruit when gentile followers of Jesus shout out in response, "The LORD *is God!*" Here we may understand "God" as a placeholder for an inexhaustible plenitude of common nouns repurposed as praise names of the Trinity, such as (in addition to those listed in an earlier chapter) "*Sat, Cit,* and *Ananda*" (Abhishiktananda); "*Dao, De, Qi*" (Paul S. Chung); "Parent Ancestor, Brother Ancestor, Holy Spirit" (Charles Nyamiti); and so on.

The Church as the Body of Christ: The Solidarity of Jew and Gentile in Praise of God the Father

Blessed be the God and Father of our Lord Jesus Christ, who . . .
destined us for adoption as his children through Jesus Christ. . . .
[God] has put all things under his feet and has made him the head
over all things for the church, which is his body. . . . He is our peace;
in his flesh he has made both groups [the "circumcision" and the
"uncircumcision"] into one and has broken down the dividing wall,
that is, the hostility between us. (Eph 1:3, 5, 22–23; 2:14)

The phrase "body of Christ" differs in an important way from the two ecclesial motifs we have already considered. Prior to the incarnation, there was already a "people of God" set aside for the glory of the Tetragrammaton—namely, the Jews. Similarly, I have argued that prior to the incarnation, the Spirit was already secretly at work among all the nations of the world preparing them to adorn the eschatological temple of God with praise. In contrast, there was no "body of Christ" prior to the incarnation. The incarnation itself is the way the second person of the Trinity acquires a human body around which the church can first be formed as his corporate body in the world. It is true that theologians such as Irenaeus perceived something like preincarnation manifestations of Christ's body in the christophanies of the Old Testament. But I think Augustine staked out a superior position when he rejected this exegetical tradition in favor of an emphasis on the unprecedented mystery of the incarnation.[24] When we designate the church the "Body of Christ," we imply that the unprecedented novelty and mystery that belongs in the first instance to the incarnation belongs in a secondary and derivative way to the church. As the corporate body is gathered and nourished by Christ's body and blood, the church exists as an extension of the incarnation and manifests it—however imperfectly—to the world.

The special place of the "body of Christ" among the three ecclesial images is mirrored to some extent by the special place of "the Father, the Son, and the Holy Spirit" among the three patterns of naming the Trinity that we identified in earlier chapters. Like the "body of Christ" as a designation for the church, the kinship vocabulary of "the Father, the Son, and the Holy Spirit" centers on the second person and illuminates the novelty and mystery of the incarnation, above all, by underscoring the reciprocity-in-the-Spirit that is revealed by Jesus's relation to the Father. To be sure, the New Testament's vocabulary of divine kinship draws on Old Testament antecedents (cf. Exod 4:22; 2 Sam 7:13–17), as Marianne Meye Thompson has shown. But Ben Witherington and Laura M. Ice are correct to insist that the New Testament also radically transforms this vocabulary by emphasizing Jesus's unique status as the Father's "only Son" (John 1:18).[25] Unlike David or the people Israel, Jesus is not first a son of Adam who becomes a son of God thanks to God's adoptive love for him. Rather, he is first the Son of God who becomes a son of Adam thanks to God's adoptive love for the world (cf. John 3:16; Luke 1:26–56; 2:1–38; 3:23–38; Gal 4:4). The Trinitarian vocabulary of divine-kinship-in-the-Spirit highlights the *novum* of the incarnation by affirming that the kinship reciprocity it reveals belongs to God's eternal identity as God.[26]

A recurrent theme of this book has been that the New Testament uses three irreducibly distinct vocabularies to express the mutuality of the three persons of the Holy Trinity. In addition to the vocabulary of kinship, the Fourth Gospel, for example, signifies the second person's eternal presence with the first by using both common nouns (John 1:1) and oblique references to the Tetragrammaton (John 8:58). Still, in this particular context, the vocabulary of divine kinship has a marked advantage over the other two vocabularies. Unlike them, it signals the eternal mutuality of the divine life "effortlessly," by virtue of the plain meaning of its root terms. In this respect, the kinship pattern of naming the Trinity does what the other patterns do in a specially pointed way.

When we combine the incarnational focus of the image of the church as the "body of Christ" with the christocentric focus of the Trinitarian vocabulary of "the Father, the Son, and the Holy

Spirit," the result is an interpretive paradigm that links Trinity and church with great power. But precisely because it is so powerful, it comes with a great danger as well: it can simply overshadow or even break loose from the other ecclesial images and patterns of Trinitarian naming altogether. When this happens, the other patterns are expelled altogether (Marcion) or allowed to remain hidden in the dark recesses of our theological imagination (as a superficial reading of the first quotation from Irenaeus at the beginning of this chapter might suggest).

To forestall this danger, it is necessary to cultivate an appreciation for the full "breadth and length and height and depth" of the mystery of the incarnation (Eph 3:18). A cardinal way of doing this is by orienting ourselves to Jesus Christ's own characteristic ways of speaking to and about God. As the Word made flesh, Jesus of Nazareth addresses the One to whom he prays using a panoply of different kinds of words: "Our Father [kinship term], hallowed be your name [proper name], your kingdom come [common noun]!" As Irenaeus recognized and Marcion did not, Jesus's address to God as "Father" opens a capacious space that includes the kinds of names that God has used to express God's goodness toward Jews and toward gentiles. Jesus's filial address is not a monoculture but one element in a differentiated ecosystem of doxology whose roots extend to eternity and whose range encompasses all human beings of every time and place (John 1:4, 9). The incarnation is the divine lexical ecosystem made flesh, as it were, for the purpose of gathering all of humanity in a differentiated ecosystem of praise.

I propose that this understanding of the incarnation should inform our understanding of what it means for the church to be the body of Christ, the prolongation of the incarnation in the world. A striking feature of the New Testament's portrait of the postresurrection Jesus movement is that it comprises Jews and gentiles who remain Jews and gentiles even as they are united to one another in Christ (cf. Acts 15, 21).[27] The "differentiated unity of Jew and gentile"[28] is such an obvious feature of the apostolic church that subsequent generations of Christians have felt the need to account for it. Writing at a time when the church had become an all but exclusively gentile institution, Jerome and Augustine held that the New Testament's portrait of the church was in effect the snapshot of a passing anomaly. Jerome held that the apostles pretended to live as Jews to avoid giving offense to their former compatriots, even though they were fully aware that their observance of the ceremonial law was not pleasing to God. Augustine, on the contrary, rejected the idea of apostolic deceit and argued that God wanted the apostolic church to consist of both those who observed the law of Moses and those who did not. Augustine maintained, however, that God willed this only for a limited period of time, after which the practice of the law became sinful. He compared the apostles' continued practice of the Mosaic law to the honor that survivors give to the bodies of the deceased before burial. After the law was properly buried, God's desire was that the body of Christ take its natural shape as a community without Jews, as Augustine understood the church to be in his own day.[29]

Jerome and Augustine recognized that the New Testament portrayed the church as a differentiated unity of Jew and gentile, but they could not imagine that this remains "a qualitative definition of the Church of the New Covenant," as the Roman Catholic document "The Gifts and the Calling of God Are Irrevocable" would maintain over a millennium and a half later. They could not, both because their understanding of the Bible's unity lacked a positive place for such a definition and because they held beliefs that actively contradicted it. Chief among these was supersessionism, the belief that the Jews are no longer the people of God, their place having been taken by the church. J. Kameron Carter and Willie James Jennings have advanced the contemporary discussion of supersessionism by showing how it has been poisonous not only for the church's relation to the Jewish people but also for the Christian social imagination generally. According to Jennings, supersessionism operates when the church imagines itself to be the graced embodiment of the creaturely universal as such while externalizing Jewish and gentile identity as merely natural, particular, outmoded, and inferior. Supersessionism so defined instantiates a diseased social imagination that over time identified the norm of redeemed humanity with the church's contingent historical expression in imperial Rome and Western European societies. In the modern era, the logic of supersessionism lives on in conceptions of Christian identity that conflate incorporation in the body of Christ with assimilation to the cultural norms of white racialized ethnonationalism.[30]

The aspect of Jennings's proposal that I want to highlight for the purposes of this chapter is the remedy that he proposes for the church's diseased social imagination. It is this: a "return to the original relationship of Jews and Gentiles" and a renewed vision "of Israel and Gentiles, of Israel and a Gentile church, of the Jewish body and the Gentile body joined."[31] The parallel between Jennings's remedy and the qualitative definition of the church proposed by "The Gifts and the Calling of God Are Irrevocable" is unmistakable. Surely the return and renewed vision that Jennings recommends are the work of generations, as is that of dismantling the wreckage wrought by supersessionism. But one aspect of that work is learning how to read the Bible as a theological unity in such a way that the apostolic church does not appear as an anomaly. That is the challenge this chapter has sought to address. In light of the ecclesiological sketch presented here, what must appear incongruous is the thought that the church has no room for an abiding distinction between Jew and gentile. As the body of Christ, the church is the temporal and spatial extension in the medium of frail human flesh of Jesus Christ its head, the incarnation of the Word of God. Just as Jesus's filial address to God as "Father" opens a capacious place that includes the names that God has used to express God's goodness toward Jew and gentile, so the church itself is not a monoculture but a differentiated ecosystem of praise that incorporates the forms of praise that Jew and gentile are providentially equipped to provide. The antiphonal call and response of "the Lᴏʀᴅ is God" and "the Lᴏʀᴅ is *God!*" to the praise of "the Father of lights" (Jas 1:17) is not a passing feature of the church's life but the luminous sign of its messianic identity in both the present age and the world to come.

The Church as *Communio* (*Koinonia*)

Robert Jenson notes that there is a motif that is even more prominent in ecumenical ecclesiology than the affirmation that the church is the people of God, the body of Christ, and the temple of the Spirit. That is the claim that the church is a communion (*koinonia, communio*). According to Jenson, the key insight of this motif is that "the communion that is now the church is itself constituted by an event of communion or participation, with the communion that is the Trinity."[32] How might we understand the relationship between these two ecumenically prominent themes? I propose that one legitimate way is this: The church is a communion in communion with the Trinity in the unity of its identity as the people of God, the body of Christ, and the temple of the Spirit. When we describe the church in these three ways, we are not describing a salvation-historical sequence, nor three Trinities and three churches, nor three parts of the Trinity and three parts of the church. We are describing the whole Trinity and the whole church three times over, each time from the perspective of the church's special bond with one person in particular. Were we to develop a communion ecclesiology along these lines, we would quickly discover that we can describe the church as *communio* only by making reference to the great majority of Jews who are not followers of Christ, for they too are the people of God, and the great majority of gentiles who likewise are not his followers, for they too participate in the Spirit's ongoing work of preparing the nations for their contributions to the doxology of the new creation. The church is *already* a communion only by *anticipation* of what it will be in the future: the ingathering of Israel *as* Israel and the nations *as* nations in the differentiated unity of the saints in the new creation, gathered around the One who sits on the throne and the Lamb (Rev 5:13, 21:22–27).

Church and World

CHRISTIANS AND JEWS

"THEY ARE ISRAELITES": THE PRIORITY OF THE
PRESENT TENSE FOR JEWISH-CHRISTIAN RELATIONS

OUR ASSESSMENT OF the significance of Romans 9–11 for the relationship between Christians and Jews depends a great deal on
whether we see it in the context of Jewish-Christian *dialogue* in the
narrower sense or Jewish-Christian *relations* in the broader sense.

So far as I am aware, Romans 9–11 is not often put on the agenda
of Jewish-Christian dialogue. This is really not too surprising. In
this passage, Paul addresses the theological quandary that arises
for him from the fact that most of his Jewish kinsmen have not
accepted the gospel of Jesus Christ. Frankly, there is not much here
for the Jewish conversation partner to grab hold of. I discovered
this for myself years ago when I was teaching a class on Romans
9–11 for Christian laity. I was a graduate student, and I was hold-
ing my class in the chaplain's office of Yale University. Unexpect-
edly, the director of the campus Hillel organization came in and
took a seat. This was entirely kosher, so to speak, because it was
understood that events held in the chaplain's office were open
to all members of the university community. Still, the rabbi's
presence changed the class dynamics in a profound way. Up to that
moment, I had succeeded in making Romans 9–11 sound fresh
and impressive to me and to my Christian audience. But Paul
sounded very different to us as soon as we knew he was also being
heard by *Jewish* ears. Now Paul sounded fiercely christocentric,
polemical, and harsh, even at his covenant-affirming best, so to
speak. And sure enough, it wasn't long before the rabbi, unable

to contain himself any longer, made crystal clear how alien and even offensive he found Paul's reasoning from beginning to end.

Yet if Romans 9–11 has fairly modest significance for Jewish-Christian *dialogue*, the same is not true, I think, for Jewish-Christian *relations*. Since 1945, the ecumenical churches have been living out a slow-motion "rediscovery" of Romans 9–11, one that invites comparison, in my view, with the Reformation's "rediscovery" of the Pauline doctrine of justification, or perhaps even with Josiah's rediscovery of the book of the law in the temple (2 Kgs 22). One palpable index of this rediscovery is the numerous official teaching documents that have been promulgated by the churches over the past two generations concerning the church's relation to Judaism.[1] These documents—by now a veritable cloud of witnesses—put the churches on record as rejecting key elements of traditional Christian teaching regarding the Jews (notably, the teaching that the church has superseded Israel as God's covenant people) and as affirming, under one form of language or another, the Jewish people's continued status as God's covenant partner, alongside the church of Jesus Christ. Significantly, these documents, however different from one another in other respects, are united in the cardinal authority they assign to passages from Romans 9–11 and, above all, to Paul's affirmation that "the gifts and the calling of God are irrevocable" (Rom 11:29). Indeed, I think it is safe to say that were Romans 9–11 not a part of the Christian canon, this change in Christian teaching could not have taken place. To be sure, numerous qualifications are in order: First, Romans 9–11 did not *occasion* this change in Christian teaching; historical events did. Second, the change itself is understood and expressed differently by different communions, seldom with anything approaching consistent fidelity to Paul's message in Romans 9–11. And third, above all, the *reception* of this change into the life and thinking of the churches is uneven, spotty, and even at times disheartening. Nevertheless, the fact remains that Romans 9–11 has served as *the* scriptural catalyst for one of the most remarkable changes in Christian teaching since the close of the conciliar era, one whose implications for

Jewish-Christian relations will continue to unfold for many generations to come.

Four Points of Enduring Relevance

Let me briefly suggest four areas where I believe Romans 9–11 has already and will continue to exert influence on Christian self-understanding in ways that make a difference for relations between Christians and Jews and, indirectly, for Jewish-Christian dialogue.[2]

The Priority of the Present Tense

The single most important element of Romans 9–11 for Jewish-Christian relations is its use of the *present tense* to characterize the Jewish people—Paul's kinsmen "according to the flesh"—as the people of God and the heirs of God's covenant promises. We encounter this all-important present tense at two crucial points—first, near the very beginning: "They *are* Israelites [οιτινες εισιν Ισραηλιται] and to them belong the adoption, the glory, the covenants, the giving of the law, the worship, and the promises; to them belong the patriarchs, and from them, according to the flesh, comes the Messiah, who is over all, God blessed forever. Amen" (Rom 9:4–5; italics added). And again near the very end (where the present tense is, to be sure, implied): "As far as the gospel is concerned, they are enemies for your sake; but as far as election is concerned, they are loved [κατα δε την εκλογην αγαπτοι] on account of the patriarchs" (11:28, NIV).

It is impossible to overstate the importance of these two present-tense passages for the structure of Paul's argument. They are the iron bookends that bracket Paul's argument and ultimately contain its explosive force, rendering it coherent, symmetrical, and whole. In Romans 9:4–5, Paul sets forth an article of faith, or *credendum*, using the present tense: "They *are* Israelites." The present tense "are" (εισιν) can be classified as a customary present that signals an ongoing state "with the temporal ends 'kicked out.'"[3] In the ensuing argument, Paul proceeds to test the truth and intelligibility of this article of faith in light of the sovereignty of the electing God (chap. 9), the gospel of Jesus Christ (chap. 10), and their mysterious interpenetration (chap. 11). In Romans 11:28, Paul returns to the original article of faith and reaffirms it in different words, stating it now in a tested and deepened form. Between statement (Rom 9:4–5) and restatement (11:28–29), the *credendum* itself (the "present tense" election of Paul's kinsmen "according to the flesh") is subjected to the most withering criticism. Indeed, the *credendum* is in a certain sense *negated* and *dissolved* as other equally binding *credenda* make their decisive contributions to Paul's investigation. Yet ultimately, Paul returns to the original article of faith and triumphantly reaffirms it, thereby motivating the doxology that concludes the section (Rom 11:33–36).

When Christians do not attend in a serious way to "the shock of the present tense" in Romans 9–11, they are prone to read their Scriptures in ways that lead them to conclude that God's election of the Jewish people was a phenomenon of the *ancient past*. Perhaps if they pay a little attention to Romans 11, they will also think of Israel's election as a phenomenon of the *eschatological future*, when "all Israel will be saved" (11:26). This traditional Christian view of Israel's election may remind us of the White Queens's attitude toward jam in *Through the Looking Glass*: "Jam yesterday, and jam tomorrow, but never jam today!"[4] Precisely here, the "shock of the present tense" in Romans 9–11 exerts its enduring, foundational importance for Christian-Jewish relations. To the degree that Christians submit themselves to this shock, they will turn to their Jewish neighbor and see one who is God's beloved, not *only* in the primordial past and eschatological future, but *also* and *above all* in the abiding *now* of covenant history. They *are* Israelites!

The Evangelical Significance of Israel's "No" to the Gospel

This brings us directly to a second point: the evangelical significance of Israel's "no" to the gospel. As we just noted, Paul's *credendum* concerning the present-tense election of gospel-rejecting Israel is affirmed in Romans 9:4–5 and reaffirmed in 11:28–29. Notice that Paul presents this *credendum* differently in each case. Initially, Paul introduces the *credendum* by assigning to *himself* the Moses- and Christlike role of the suffering mediator on behalf of his people: "For I could wish that *I myself* were accursed and cut off from Christ for the sake of *my own people*, my kindred according to the flesh. They are Israelites" (Rom 9:3–4a; italics added).

Ultimately, however, Paul assigns the role of suffering mediator *to Israel herself in her gospel-rejecting condition*, on behalf of the gentile followers of Christ Jesus: "As far as the gospel is concerned, they are enemies *for your sake*; but as far as election is concerned, they are loved on account of the patriarchs" (11:28, NIV; italics added).

This reassignment of roles *from* the apostle Paul *to* gospel-rejecting Israel (!) is a key part of the "theological harvest" that Paul reaps by the end of Romans 11. It is all the more important for two reasons. First, the mediating role that Paul originally wished to claim for himself was only hypothetical, whereas the mediating role that he ultimately assigns to Israel is real, not contrary to fact. Second, Paul makes clear that this mediatorial role comes to Israel from God's own hand: "A hardening has come upon part of Israel, until the full number of the Gentiles has come in" (Rom 11:25). Therefore, Israel's "no" is God's doing, together, of course, with the humiliation it entails (e.g., "stumbling" [11:12], "rejection" [11:15], "defeat" [11:13]). It is, so to speak, an evangelical no, insofar as God has assimilated Israel's fate to Christ's passion *for the sake of the gospel itself.*

The divinely ordained character of Israel's "no" to the gospel has two important consequences.

First, it reinforces the point that gentile Christians have *no* apostolic commission to try to win the Jewish people to faith in Christ Jesus by means of direct proclamation. I say *reinforce* because such a commission is not contemplated anywhere else in the New Testament either, so far as I can see. In any case, Paul explicitly excludes such a commission when he traces back the de facto failure of direct mission to the Jews (Rom 10:14–21) to God's "hardening" (11:25). The only form of mission toward the Jewish people that Paul holds open to his gentile audience is the *indirect* one that Paul implies in Romans 11:13–14, according to which the church of the gentiles is to provoke Israel to "jealousy," presumably because of the richness and clarity with which it displays the fruits of life in the Spirit. This indirect mission strategy, we may safely say, remains too little explored, even after two thousand years.

Second, Paul rests his hope for the ultimate salvation of gospel-rejecting Israel not on the church's missionary efforts but on God-in-Christ's direct intervention on Israel's behalf at the end of the age: "And *so* all Israel will be saved. . . . *Out of Zion* will come the Deliverer; *he* will banish ungodliness from Jacob" (Rom 11:26; italics added). As Bertold Klappert has observed, this future event is "trans-kerygmatic" and "trans-ecclesiological."[5] It does not depend on the mediation of the church or its kerygma. This means that the church does not come ever nearer to God's kingdom the more Jews it "converts," or even the more vividly it models life in the Spirit. Rather, both the church and Israel are separated from God's eschatological reign by a hiatus, a hiatus that can be filled only by the Lord's redemptive and healing advent on behalf of all Israel, and most particularly, on behalf of gospel-rejecting, carnal Israel, God's beloved whom God has made to participate for a season in the humiliations of the Messiah and Son of God for the sake of the world's salvation.

Covenant History as the Sitz im Leben of the Church

One way to begin to draw out some of the systematic implications of the previous points is to say that according to Romans 9–11, covenant history remains the living context—the *Sitz im Leben*, if you like—of the church's life: past, present, and future.

By covenant history, I mean God's sovereign rule over all history as the God of Israel—that is, as the God who has called the people of Israel by name in a way in which God has not called any other nation or people (cf. Deut 7:7). A key feature of covenant history is the nations' *dependence* on God's fidelity toward *Israel* as a condition of the nations' own eschatological blessing (cf. Gen 12:1–5;

Gal 3:14). When the Christian canon is read *apart* from Romans 9–11, it seems as though covenant history has been completed *post Christum natum* and now belongs to the past. According to such a reading, the old distinction between Jew and gentile, between Israel and nations, has been superseded by the new distinction between *church and world*, which dissolves the older pair into itself. As covenant history recedes into the past, so too does the gentiles' *dependence* on God's fidelity to the election of Israel, as well as Israel's vocation to be God's people in the midst of the nations. All this becomes the form of our *memory*, not of our present experience and of our future expectation.

In Romans 9–11, covenant history returns with a vengeance. More accurately, we must say that covenant history surges into the *foreground* of Paul's letter in a way that demonstrates that it was never really absent from the *background*, whether in the previous chapters Romans 5–8 or, indeed, anywhere elsewhere in the letter. A key measure of the renewed visibility of covenant history in Romans 9–11 is the fact that Paul never speaks of the *church* or of the *saints* but rather of Jews and gentiles, Israel and the nations, irrespective of whether he is speaking of the past, present, or future, or of those who are or are not believers in Christ Jesus. To be sure, Paul invokes the distinction between Jew and gentile partly in order to *interrogate* its legitimacy on the basis of the sovereignty of God (Rom 9:6–33) and "the righteousness that comes from faith" (10:6). But ultimately, Paul's interrogation of the distinction leads not to its dissolution but rather to the discovery that *the gentiles' dependence on God's fidelity to Israel remains in force, even in the present topsy-turvy day*: "Now I am speaking to you Gentiles. . . . Remember that it is not you that support the root, but the root that supports you" (Rom 11:13a, 18).

For Christians accustomed to thinking of themselves in terms of the church/world paradigm, Paul's words are profoundly *decentering*. Gentile Christians are jolted awake with the discovery that they *are*—not just *were*—gentile Christians, with the discovery that they *are*—not just *were*—dependent on God's fidelity to a people *other than themselves*. In this connection, we can recall Paul's climactic words toward the end of the letter, noting in particular Paul's use of the perfect tense, denoting a completed action that continues *into the present*: "For I tell you that Christ *has become* [γεγενῆσθαι] a servant of the circumcised on behalf of the truth of God in order that he might confirm the promises given to the patriarchs, and in order that the Gentiles might glorify God for his mercy. As it is written, 'Therefore I will confess you among the Gentiles, and sing praises to your name'" (Rom 15:8–9; italics added).

In sum, Romans 9–11 drives home a truth that concerns the letter as a whole: God's sovereignty over history as the God of Israel does not merely *prepare* for the church. It *surrounds* and *infuses* the church as its perpetual context, as the blessed medium of its own evangelical existence.

YHWH, the Name of the God of Israel

In the passage I just quoted, Paul cites Psalm 18:49: "Therefore I will confess you among the Gentiles, and sing praises to your name" (Rom 15:9).

What is the praiseworthy name Paul alludes to here? In its original setting in Psalm 18, the phrase "your name" refers to the Tetragrammaton, God's personal proper name. To this day, Jews regard the Tetragrammaton as *the* sacred name of God, and they single it out (as the New Testament writers do) by the practice of nonpronunciation. Christians, on the other hand, have a much more ambivalent attitude toward the Tetragrammaton. They often treat it as a name that tells us who God *was* but no longer who God *is* and who God *will be*—these functions having been taken over by new names, such as "Jesus" and "the Father, the Son, and the Holy Spirit." Perhaps for this reason, Christians outside the setting of worship often fail to honor the Tetragrammaton by avoiding its pronunciation, despite the precedent set by their own Scriptures.

At just this point, Romans 9–11 asserts its significance once again. To the degree that Christians take Romans 9–11 seriously, they will, I believe, be prodded to recognize that the praiseworthy name of Romans 15:8 is in fact none other than YHWH, the name of the God of Israel.

As has often been noted, Romans 9–11 is dense with citations of Scripture. These citations have their center of gravity not in Israel's election, nor even in the gospel of justification, but in the divine "I."[6] By my count, the divine "I" comes to expression no fewer than *twenty-seven times* in Romans 9–11: ten times through the use of personal pronouns (I, me, my) and seventeen times through verbal conjugations.[7] For Paul, of course, the divine "I" of Romans 9–11 is not a *nameless* subject, a naked will, but *YHWH*, the living Deity of covenant history. This is demonstrated by Paul's repeated citation of YHWH texts (scriptural passages in which the Divine Name appears in Hebrew manuscripts) over the course of the argument, as follows:

9:1–5	Paul's lament for the Israelites and praise for God's gifts to them
9:6–29	God's calling of Israel and the nature of election
9:27–29	Two YHWH texts ascribed to God
9:30–10:21	Israel's failure explained
10:13	One YHWH text ascribed to Christ
11:1–32	God's use of Israel's failure and ultimate vindication of God's gifts to Israel
11:33–36	Hymn of adoration
11:33	One YHWH text ascribed to God

In view of Paul's repeated citation of YHWH texts and the prominence of the divine "I," we might say that Romans 9–11 is, in a certain sense, a meditation on the meaning of the name "YHWH." The urgency of the meditation arises from the fact that this name gives rise to two apparently contradictory *credenda*: God's fidelity to God's promises to Paul's kinsmen *kata sarka* and the gospel of justification by faith. Paul's meditation comes to a conclusion with the discovery that both *credenda* are, we might say, different but complimentary ways of paraphrasing the Divine Name. (The

Lord's own original paraphrase for the Divine Name appears in Exod 34:6–7 and reads, in part, "The LORD, the LORD, a God merciful and gracious, slow to anger, and abounding in steadfast love and faithfulness.") For Paul, the meaning of the Divine Name can, with equal aptness, be paraphrased with the words "Jesus is Lord" (Rom 10:9) and with the words "the gifts and the calling of God are irrevocable" (Rom 11:29).

While these two "paraphrases of the Divine Name" initially *appear to be* contradictory, ultimately, they are understood in and through each other. Christ Jesus *confirms* God's promises to the patriarchs (Rom 15:8), and God's faithfulness to Israel transpires through its assimilation to Christ's own rejection and humiliation for the sake of the world's salvation (Rom 11:12). It is for this reason that Paul concludes Romans 9–11 with a doxology that acknowledges both the *graciousness* and the *unsupersedability* of God's identity as the bearer of the Divine Name: "'For who has known the mind of the Lord? Or who has been his counselor?' 'Or who has given a gift to him, to receive a gift in return?' For from him and through him and to him are all things. To him be the glory *forever*. Amen" (Rom 11:34–46; italics added).

Conclusion

I began by suggesting that Jewish-Christian *dialogue* is too narrow a framework to assess the theological significance of Romans 9–11. But in the end, Jewish-Christian *relations* are also too narrow. Ultimately, Romans 9–11 is theologically significant because it propels gentile Christians to recognize that God's irrevocable calling of the Jewish people is an internal, essential, and perpetual dimension of their own identity as Christians.[8]

8

CHRISTIANITY, JUDAISM, AND ISLAM

THE SIGN OF JONAH: A CHRISTIAN PERSPECTIVE
ON THE RELATION OF THE ABRAHAMIC FAITHS

The Abrahamic Religions?

JUDAISM, CHRISTIANITY, AND Islam are frequently spoken of as "the Abrahamic religions." This is certainly justified insofar as each tradition traces its origins back to Abraham in one fashion or another. Yet it would be a mistake to think that Abraham represents a simple common denominator among the three traditions, a ready point of convergence and common ground, as it were. As Jon Levenson has shown, each tradition conceives of Abraham in its own image, making the patriarch it remembers and honors as irreducibly particular as the traditions themselves.[1]

The distinctiveness of the traditions asserts itself once again when one considers how each tradition conceives of its relationship to the other two "Abrahamic" faiths. Martin S. Jaffee has proposed that the three religions are all instances of a common type of elective monotheism, with the consequence that the three religions all employ the same basic pattern to understand religions other than themselves.[2] According to this view, it would seem that the relation of the three faiths could be plotted as a sequence of successive supersessions: Judaism purports to supersede paganism and idolatry, Christianity to supersede Judaism, and Islam to supersede both Christianity and Judaism. Yet even this picture remains too simple, for it suggests that the meaning of supersessionism is the same in each instance. It fails to reckon with the fact that "superseding" may take different shapes in each tradition and

145

may not represent an equally imperative feature of each tradition's self-understanding.[3]

In reality, each of the three religions conceives of its relationship to the other two faiths in ways that are distinctive to it its own character and scriptural sources. For this reason, there cannot be "an Abrahamic theology of the Abrahamic faiths," as if there were a single common core that we could drill down to in our reflection on the three traditions. Instead, there can only be a more complicated reality: a Jewish theology of Judaism in relation to Christianity and Islam, a Christian theology of Christianity in relation to Judaism and Islam, a Muslim theology of Islam in relation to Judaism and Christianity.

As a Christian theologian, it is not for me to write a Jewish or Muslim theology of anything, of course. But I can attempt to sketch a Christian understanding of Christianity's relationship to Judaism and Islam, which is what I want to do in this chapter. Right off the bat, however, I am faced with a fact that makes this a particularly difficult challenge. Christianity relates to the other two Abrahamic faiths in profoundly asymmetrical ways. The root of this asymmetry is not hard to see. Christianity shares with Judaism a common body of sacred Scripture. It does not do so with Islam.[4] The scriptural imperative that forces Christians to reckon with how the Jewish people figure in God's purposes (cf. Rom 9–11) has no counterpart that forces it to reckon with Islam in a similar way, nor does it provide obvious resources for doing so.

To this first difficulty we can add another. While Christianity has developed over time a variety of categories for understanding competing religious movements, Islam does not seem to fit neatly into any of them. I list a few such categories with brief accounts of why Islam does not seem to fit:

Paganism. Islam came into being as a proclamation of the one God against polytheism; hence it can hardly be classified as an instance of the kind of religion against which, for example, Isaiah and Paul polemicize.

Heresy. John of Damascus and other early Christian writers classified Islam along with the rival forms of Christianity that they considered to be heresies. Eventually, however, Christians concluded that Islam was not a heretical distortion of its own teaching but a separate "religion" in its own right.

Non-Christian Religion. The Second Vatican Council in *Nostra Aetate* employed this category as the major heading for its discussion of Christianity in relation to the world faiths, including Islam. However broad and bland, it would seem to have the merit of descriptive accuracy. Yet in fact, the council's decision to locate all major religions under this heading is problematic, most obviously so in the case of Judaism, since it takes no account of the uniquely intimate nature of the relation between Christianity and Judaism. Similarly, however, there is an important sense in which Islam is not a "non-Christian" religion in the same way as, for example, Hinduism and Buddhism. Unlike other non-Christian religions, Islam venerates Jesus of Nazareth and, indeed, accords to him a unique prophetic dignity that in some respects seems to exceed even that of Muhammed himself.

Natural Revelation. Finally, it is not easy to locate Islam using the distinction of natural and special revelation. Christians might be drawn to employ the former category as a way of acknowledging the spiritual and moral wisdom embodied in Islam without accepting its self-description as a continuation of God's revelation through the tradition of biblical prophets. Moreover, this designation might also seem appropriate because Islam has characterized itself as *din al-fitra*—the original, natural religion of humanity. Yet counting against this is again the fact that Islam makes central to its own self-understanding the figures and events that for Christians belong to the very essence of special revelation, such as, for example, Abraham, Moses, David, Mary, and Jesus.

One could test other categories, but I suspect the result would be much the same. Perhaps, however, this negative result provides a clue for the distinctive shape of a Christian theology of

Judaism and Islam. Both Judaism and Islam exact from Christianity a recognition of their respective uniquenesses and irreducibilities, although in very different ways. Judaism does so by virtue of being in some sense an integral dimension of Christian faith in a way that differentiates it from all other religions, including Islam. Islam does so as a religion that in its distinctive mix of the familiar and strange resists interpretation within ready categories of Christian comprehension, whether positive or negative.

Speaking in Parables

So far, I have explained why it is difficult to develop a Christian theology of the Abrahamic faiths on the basis of Scripture. Now I want to suggest a way in which it might be possible to do this: by interpreting Scripture typologically. Typology refers to the interpretation of persons, events, and relationships—including those that are *not* explicitly mentioned in Scripture—in light of their resemblance or correspondence to persons, events, and relationships that *are* explicitly mentioned in Scripture.[5] The Christian canon does not explicitly address the church's relationship to Judaism and Islam. Nevertheless, a typological reading of Scripture can try to illuminate this relationship by exploring how it resembles or corresponds to other biblically attested relationships.

For the purposes of this experiment (for that is how I wish this chapter to be understood), I propose turning to the book of Jonah. Jonah is a natural and instructive choice for several reasons.

In the Scriptures of Judaism, the book of Jonah is found among the prophets, a location fully warranted by many features of the book beginning with its opening line: "Now the word of the Lord came to Jonah son of Amittai, saying, 'Go at once to Nineveh'" (Jonah 1:1–2). In literary terms, however, the book is the canon's purest example of an extended parable. The story invites the reader to understand it not only as the account of the misadventures of one wayward prophet but as a riddle/satire/commentary on Israel's vocation as God's people in the midst of the nations. The simple but enigmatic plot raises themes of enduring relevance, such as the relation of divine judgment and mercy, of insiders and outsiders, of repentance and obedience, and more. Yet to tap that relevance, the story must be unriddled time and again and connected to new circumstances and problems. Typological interpretation is not the only way to do this, but it is, I believe, a legitimate way.

In the New Testament, the Gospels record that Jesus used typological interpretation to apply the story of Jonah to himself and his ministry. Some of the priests and Pharisees, we read, demanded that Jesus perform a miracle to prove that he was acting with divine authority. In response to their demand, Jesus replied, "An evil and adulterous generation asks for a sign, but no sign will be given to it except the sign of the prophet Jonah. For just as Jonah was three days and three nights in the belly of the sea monster, so for three days and three nights the Son of Man will be in the heart of the earth. The people of Nineveh will rise up at the judgment with this generation and condemn it, because they repented at the proclamation of Jonah, and see, something greater than Jonah is here!" (Matt 12:39–41).

The saying illustrates a general feature of typological interpretation. A correspondence is drawn between selected details of the scriptural story (Jonah, the whale, and the repentance of the Ninevites) and contemporary reality (Jesus, his death and resurrection, and "this generation"), with the result that the two sets of affairs are now understood in light of each other. At the same time, the saying illustrates something distinctive about *Christian* typological interpretation. In this example, Jesus does not treat the ancient canonical story as the "greater" or weightier pole of the interpretive relationship, as one might expect. Rather, he does the reverse. Jesus presents himself, in all his novelty and immediacy, as the *greater* thing that the story of Jonah foreshadows. In this, Jesus sets the pattern for all subsequent Christian interpretation. In time, Christians came to regard this story and other early witnesses to Jesus as sacred writings on par with the Hebrew Bible, thereby creating a two-part canon of Old and New Testaments. Once this happened, however, Christians did not then repeat the process by looking for *still greater* realities in relation to which Jesus is one type among others. Rather, they continued to understand Jesus Christ as the unique and unsurpassable center of all typological interpretation. Jesus is for Christians not only the King of kings but the Clue of clues. He is the bearer of signification whose infinite density allows every other state of affairs to come alive as a type that bears witness to truth.

On this christological foundation, Christians cultivated the art of typological interpretation up until the modern era, not least with reference to the figure of Jonah. A first example comes from Saint Irenaeus (ca. 120–200):

> [God] patiently suffered Jonah to be swallowed by the whale, not that he should be swallowed up and perish altogether, but that, having been cast out again, he might be the more subject to God, and might glorify Him the more who had conferred upon him such an unhoped-for deliverance. . . . So also, from the beginning, did God permit man to be swallowed up by the great whale, who was the author of transgression, not that he should perish altogether when so engulphed; but, arranging and preparing the plan of salvation, which was accomplished by the Word, through the sign of Jonah, . . . [so] that man, receiving an unhoped-for salvation from God, might rise from the dead, and glorify God, and repeat that word which was uttered in prophecy by Jonah: "I cried by reason of mine affliction to the Lord my God, and He heard me out of the belly of hell."[6]

With simple bold strokes, Irenaeus draws a correspondence between God's conduct toward Jonah and God's conduct toward all humankind from creation to consummation. Just as God permitted Jonah's woes in order to bring him by way of "unhoped-for deliverance" to the glorification of God, so also has God permitted humankind's. The consummate mastery of Irenaeus's art is visible in how he combines literary invention (e.g., Jonah = humankind) with fidelity to both the details and the deep patterns of Scripture.

A second example comes from Saint Augustine of Hippo: "As to Jonah's building for himself a booth, and sitting down over against Nineveh, waiting to see what would befall the city, the prophet was here in his own person the symbol of another fact. He prefigured the carnal people of Israel. For he also was grieved at the salvation of the Ninevites, that is, at the redemption and deliverance of the Gentiles, from among whom Christ came to call, not righteous men, but sinners to repentance."[7]

Augustine goes on to offer a detailed interpretation of the vine that grows up to shelter Jonah, only to be stricken by a worm and die. The vine represents the earthly privileges that God gave to the Jewish nation during the Old Testament dispensation. The worm that devours the vine is Christ. With his mouth, Christ openly proclaims the gospel, which was formerly foreshadowed by Israel's earthly benefits, but by doing so, he causes these benefits to lose their significance and wither away. The Jewish nation is deprived of her former glories and cast into dispersion and captivity, so that she, like Jonah, has nothing to shelter her from the "grievous heat of tribulation."[8] Augustine concludes with a final typological gloss on the last verses of the book: "Nevertheless, the salvation of the Gentiles and of the penitent is of more importance in the sight of God than this sorrow of Israel and the 'shadow' of which the Jewish nation was so glad."[9]

Augustine's interpretation is brilliant and troubling. He proves beyond a doubt that typological interpretation, harnessed to the book of Jonah, provides Christians with an uncommonly powerful tool for making Christian sense of religious outsiders— in this case, Jews. But he also illustrates the dangers that come with that power. A book written to teach Jews that God is merciful to gentiles becomes by the power of typology a book that teaches gentile Christians that God has abandoned the Jews! A Christian theologian writing today may well wish to learn from Augustine's skill as a typologist without accepting his belief that Christ's coming makes God's covenant with the Jews obsolete and God's faithfulness toward them as a people null and void. He or she may take comfort in the fact that Augustine, with typical modesty, does not insist on his own interpretation. He goes on to write, "Any one is at liberty to open up with a different interpretation all the other particulars which are hidden in the symbolical history of the prophet Jonah, if only it be in harmony with the rule of faith."[10]

To that task I now turn.

Jonah and Three Vectors of Conversion to the God of Abraham

Despite its brevity, the book of Jonah is a marvel of literary and theological intricacy. Like other prophetic texts, the book is concerned with the meaning of conversion to the God of Abraham. But Jonah may be distinctive by setting forth at least three different models of what such conversion means. They are as follows:

- the sailors' conversion (chap. 1)
- the Ninevites' conversion (chap. 3)
- Jonah's conversion (chaps. 2 and 4)

A careful reading of Jonah reveals that these three vectors of conversion differ significantly from one another. While they all entail a given character (or group of characters) undergoing a transformation toward greater knowledge of and obedience toward God, the transformation is notably different in each case. One way the text signals these differences is by its careful use of different names for God depending on the theological perspective of the character in question. Jonah, for example, is closely associated with the name "YHWH," the personal proper name of Israel's God. The Ninevites, in contrast, are closely associated with the appellative name "Elohim" (God), while the sailors are associated with a plurality of deities (gods). As we shall see, the text signals what each character's conversion entails (and does not entail) by the way each character learns (or does not learn) to combine these names.

My typological experiment consists in exploring a simple set of correspondences. I propose that the sailors' conversion corresponds principally to Christianity, the Ninevites' principally to Islam, and Jonah's principally to Judaism (although, as we shall see, secondarily to Christianity and perhaps also to Islam as well). I particularly want to suggest that the book of Jonah's sophisticated "name theology" provides Christians with a fruitful way of thinking about Christianity's relation to the other two Abrahamic faiths. But I happily admit that I am intrigued by how far the typological resemblances can be pushed in other respects as well.

The Sailors' Conversion: A Type of Christianity

The first thing to note about the sailors' conversion is that it results from their being caught up in somebody else's drama. The story's principals are YHWH and his servant Jonah. YHWH commissions Jonah to go to a distant city to prophecy its imminent destruction, but Jonah boards a ship and flees in the opposite direction. Intent on getting Jonah to obey, YHWH engulfs the ship in a violent storm, hapless sailors and all.

Up to this point, the story identifies the Deity exclusively by the name "YHWH," the personal name revealed to the Israelites through Moses at the time of the exodus (Exod 3:15). This corresponds to the fact that the central actors in the story so far—YHWH and Jonah—are both privy to YHWH's intimate covenantal bond with Israel. As soon as the sailors start to act as characters in their own right, however, a new term appears: "Then the mariners were afraid, and each cried to his god [*elohayw*]" (Jonah 1:5).[11] The root word in question, *elohim*, is a common noun that refers to the general class of deities. It is also used commonly in the Bible as a name or title for God, the one true Deity. In this respect, *elohim* is like the English word *god*, which may also be used as a name for the Deity (God) or to refer to the class of purported deities (the gods). In the case of the sailors' cries for divine help, it is this second usage that comes into play. The mariners, we are given to understand, are a typically international lot, each cultivating the worship of his own native deity. When their pleas prove useless, however, they awaken the sleeping Jonah and demand to know who he is. Jonah answers, "I am a Hebrew. . . . I worship YHWH, the God [*elohe*, also cognate to *elohim*] of heaven, who made the sea and the dry land" (Jonah 1:9). Jonah's reply marks the first time in the book that the personal name YHWH is linked to the more general designation "Elohim." This signals one of the book's major concerns: YHWH is also Elohim, God of the whole earth. As we shall see a bit later, Jonah's conversion consists in large part in learning to accept the full dimensions of the second half of this equation. As for the sailors, however, their discovery runs in the other direction. Having called fruitlessly upon their gods, they now come to the frightening realization that their fate is in the hands of a hitherto unknown deity named YHWH. After exhausting all other recourse, the sailors offer a moving appeal for understanding and (with Jonah's consent) throw him overboard. The raging seas grow calm. "Then the men feared YHWH even more, and they offered a sacrifice to YHWH and made vows" (Jonah 1:16).

This story, I suggest, may be understood as a type of the distinctively Christian form of conversion to the God of Abraham. More exactly, it corresponds to a distinctively *gentile* Christian form of conversion. Gentile Christians encounter the God of Israel in medias res, long after the plot of salvation history was first set into motion. The plot's narrative tension arises from the fact that YHWH previously called Jonah/Israel by name for a purpose that also includes the benefit of the nations (Gen 12:1–5; Jonah 1:1–2). The plot comes to a climax in a dramatic act of divine deliverance. YHWH rescues the gentiles through the obedient suffering of one Israelite, Jonah/Jesus, whom YHWH also vindicates by rescuing from doom. Delivered from death by somebody else's deity, gentile Christians learn to use the word *god* in a new way. They cease to call upon the names of their native gods, even as they learn to call upon YHWH as the one God of heaven and earth.

With only a slightly greater exercise of typological imagination, I think, the story may also be understood to foreshadow a danger spot intrinsic to the character of gentile Christianity that has continuously proven to be the occasion of its theological lapses. While the book of Jonah makes clear that the mariners learned to fear and worship YHWH as a great god of storm and sea, it gives no indication that they gave up the worship of their native deities. When Jonah said, "I worship YHWH, the God [Elohim] of heaven, who made the sea and the dry land" (1:9), it is quite possible that he meant one thing while the sailors understood another. Jonah was proclaiming YHWH to be the one God and Creator of all things (Gen 1:1), but the sailors, we may infer, simply ranged YHWH among the other gods they knew and worshipped as occasion required. The danger foreshadowed is clear. Christianity is a cosmopolitan faith, composed of many nations and united by no common tongue or culture other than their experience of salvation through YHWH and his servant Jesus (whose name means "YHWH saves"). But precisely so, gentile Christians from various lands have often sought to merge their faith in YHWH with those of their national deities, contrary to the clear testimony of the prophets and apostles. The results have proven disastrous more than once.

The Ninevites' Conversion: A Type of Islam
In Nineveh at last, Jonah prophecies the city's imminent destruction, just as he was commissioned. But the city repents and God spares it after all. Thus we have a second model of conversion to the God of Abraham. It differs from the first in several ways.

Most strikingly, the object of the Ninevites' belief and repentance is identified not by the personal name "YHWH" but rather consistently by the appellative name "Elohim." This is evident not in the reported content of Jonah's preaching (which does not mention the Deity at all; cf. "Forty days more, and Nineveh shall be overthrown" [Jonah 3:4]) but in the following verses:

> And the people of Nineveh believed God [Elohim]; they proclaimed a fast, and everyone, great and small, put on sackcloth. (Jonah 3:5)

Then he [the king] had a proclamation made in Nineveh:
". . . All shall turn from their evil ways and from the violence that is in their hands. Who knows? God may relent
and change his mind; he may turn from his fierce anger,
so that we do not perish." (Jonah 3:7–9)

The name "YHWH," it seems, does not figure in the Ninevites'
conversion at all! As if to underscore this surprising point, the narrator concludes the chapter very differently than he had begun
it. The chapter began in classical prophetic fashion: "The word of
YHWH came to Jonah a second time, saying, 'Get up, go to Nineveh,
that great city, and proclaim to it the message that I tell you'" (Jonah
3:1–2). The narrator thereby invites his audience to share in Jonah's
privileged knowledge that everything that will follow comes at
the behest of YHWH, the God of Israel. But the narrator forces his
readers to share in Jonah's surprise by ending the chapter with the
words "when God [Elohim!] saw what they did, how they turned
from their evil ways, God changed his mind about the calamity
that he had said he would bring upon them; and he did not do it"
(3:10). For the first time since the beginning of the book, the narrator designates the Deity as "Elohim," not as "YHWH"! The narrator
thereby instructs the audience that the Deity bears the name "Elohim" with as much propriety as the name "YHWH."

This story, I suggest, may be understood as a type of the distinctively Islamic form of conversion to the God of Abraham. The
most basic Muslim creed, known as the Shahadah (the Confession), declares, "There is no 'god' (*la illaha*) except God (*ill-allah*)."
This, together with the profession that Muhammed is the envoy of
Allah, is often said to form the core of the Muslim religion. In this
creed, the Tetragrammaton, the personal name of the God of Abraham, plays no role, nor indeed, as far as I am aware, does it play any
role in Muslim faith whatsoever. For Muslims, "Allah" is the name
that functions in piety and liturgy as the Deity's personal name. Ety-
mologically, however, the name shares the same Semitic root as the
Hebrew common nouns *el* (god) and *elohim*.[12] Of all the attributes

commonly ascribed by Muslims to Allah, none are more common and central than "the merciful, the compassionate," and no duties are regarded as more binding on the Muslim than the practice of piety ("They proclaimed a fast, and everyone, great and small, put on sackcloth" [Jonah 3:5]) and the turning away from wickedness (cf. the king's decree: "All shall turn from their evil ways and from the violence that is in their hands" [Jonah 3:8]).

Another point of typological correspondence: Soon after Jonah arrives in Nineveh, his role and his message are over-shadowed by the religious initiative taken by the Ninevites them-selves and, above all, by the king, who issues a binding religious proclamation of his own. Although occasioned by Jonah's message, the theological content of the king's proclamation is clearly differ-ent from Jonah's, and even contradictory to it, at least at a surface level. Jonah had foretold doom, but the king reasons, "Who knows? God may relent" (Jonah 3:9). Even though the reader understands that the king is not a prophet in the same fashion as Jonah him-self, the story rates the value of the royal proclamation very high. For in the event, it is the king's message rather than Jonah's that is fulfilled according to the letter. Jonah is thereby exposed to the fate of being regarded as a false prophet—exactly the outcome, he later protests, that caused him to flee to Tarshish in the first place. In a deeper sense, however, the word given to him by YHWH has had the effect that YHWH intended. YHWH's aim was not to authenti-cate Jonah's prophetic credentials but to call a great city from wick-edness and save it from destruction. This point is key to the whole story, and we will return to it later.

Muslims regard the Qur'an as the clearest, most complete, and most authoritative revelation of God and believe it super-sedes its predecessors, and they regard Muhammed as God's final prophet. Christians cannot share these beliefs; if they did, they would cease to be Christians and would become Muslims instead. But if Christians embrace the typological reading of Jonah that I have proposed, they will nevertheless guard themselves against thinking meanly of the place of Muhammed and the Qur'an in God's mysterious providence among the nations. The king responds to Jonah's message by interposing himself—or, more exactly, his proclamation—between the Hebrew prophet and the Ninevites. Similarly, Muhammed responded to the biblical traditions known to him by interposing himself—or, more exactly, the Qur'an—between those same traditions and his audience. The result was a massive transposition of the biblical message into a new and markedly different key. But if Christians are guided by the typological reading of Jonah that I suggest, they will recognize that the sacred writing that results from this transposition possesses a truth and validity of its own, which Christians can recognize above all in the fruits of piety to which it gives rise but also in its naming of God and the honor that it accords to teachers of righteousness. Furthermore, Christians will want to guard against the assumption that wherever the Qur'an differs from the letter of biblical revelation, it is therefore false, for it may be congruent with the compassionate purpose of the God of the Bible in a way that the letter of biblical condemnation is not.

Finally, Christians may find it possible to interpret certain details of this story in a way that foreshadows what Christians may regard as a danger spot intrinsic to the character of Islam that may prove to be the occasion of its theological lapses. However true and fruitful the king's proclamation may be, the king could not have issued it had not God persisted in calling Jonah as his prophet and had not Jonah ultimately obeyed God. Yet it is only too much in the character of kings to minimize or even forget and deny such indebtedness. Perhaps Islam, too, is at times prone to overestimate its self-sufficiency and to minimize what it owes to biblical revelation generally and to Judaism in particular. Such a diagnosis, I must emphasize, reflects a Christian evaluation of Islam based on a Christian reading of the story of the book of Jonah. Nevertheless, it may be that this "outsider's" perspective is not wholly without value for Muslims. It may provide an occasion for Muslims to explore the extent to which Muslim self-understanding allows for the Qur'an to be interpreted with reference to and in light of biblical revelation as contained in the Old and New Testaments.

Jonah's Conversion: A Type of Judaism

Jonah's conversion is the book's main theme, in relation to which the other two are episodes. The book begins with YHWH adopting a personal intimacy toward Jonah that outstrips anything that the sailors or the Ninevites ever enjoy, an intimacy that has only been intensified by the book's end. The intimacy is reciprocated from Jonah's side. At the beginning of the book, Jonah can truthfully say that he worships "YHWH, the God [Elohim] of heaven, who made the sea and the dry land" (Jonah 1:9). At the end of the book, he can truthfully say that he "knew that you are a gracious God [Elohim] and merciful, slow to anger, and abounding in steadfast love, and ready to relent from punishing" (Jonah 4:2; cf. Exod 34:6–7). Where then is there room for Jonah to undergo any experience of conversion, of transformation toward God?

There is room with respect to Jonah's obedience. Along this vector, Jonah's conversion is complete by the end of the book. At first, Jonah is unwilling to accept YHWH's commission, but by the book's end, he has not only accepted but fulfilled it. But there is room for Jonah to experience transformation toward God in another way as well. And that is with respect to Jonah's capacity to understand and internalize—rather than merely profess—what it means that YHWH is *the God of heaven and earth*, not only with respect to its implications for his own reputation, but with respect to its implications for the well-being of others. This vector of conversion is still open at the book's end, at least so far as Jonah himself is concerned. But the author of the book finds a subtle way to invite his audience to absorb the point that Jonah finds so hard to swallow, once again through the sophisticated use of divine names. Throughout the book, as we have seen, the narrator has referred to the Deity either as "YHWH" or as "Elohim," depending on context. Occasionally, the two names are placed in apposition, as in Jonah's cry from the whale: "You brought up my life from the Pit, O YHWH my God [Elohim]" (Jonah 2:6). But toward the close of the book, the author brings these two names into an even more intimate connection, for the first and only time in the story: "Then YHWH God appointed a bush, and made it come up over Jonah, to give shade over his head, to save him from his discomfort; so Jonah was very happy about the bush" (Jonah 4:6).

The odd double-barreled name "YHWH God" (YHWH Elohim) is something of a rarity in the Bible. In fact, there is only one extended passage where it is used consistently as the Deity's primary designation, and that is in the Bible's first two chapters, which tell of God's dealings with humankind in the garden of Eden (Gen 2–3). There, for example, we find the following verse: "And YHWH God planted a garden in Eden, in the east; and there he put the man whom he had formed" (Gen 2:8).

The name "YHWH God," with its evocation of God's bountiful care for the whole human family, contains everything that Jonah has yet to learn to complete his conversion. As I noted, the end of the book portrays Jonah's conversion toward YHWH God as incomplete, if not stalled. Yet I do not think we are therefore entitled to assume that the story means to imply Jonah's *ultimate* incorrigibility. After all, Jonah "came around" once before. Rather, I believe we should interpret the ending of the story as a sign that YHWH God's history with Jonah is not yet finished.

This story, I suggest, may be understood as a type of the distinctively Jewish form of conversion to the God of Abraham. Of the three Abrahamic faiths, Judaism stands in a uniquely intimate relationship with YHWH God. But it has been called to this position not for its own benefit exclusively but also to serve YHWH God's love and care for the whole world. This is not an especially easy role to accept and to play, certainly not in all its dimensions. Perhaps this very difficulty is part of what the book signals by leaving Jonah's conversion still open at the end of the book.

But while I propose that Jonah's conversion is primarily a type of Judaism, I think Christians can and should apply it to themselves too, especially as a guide for thinking about their relationship to the other two religions. There is an obvious danger in finding oneself typologically represented in the book of Jonah by everyone except Jonah himself (Augustine's typology illustrates that danger). Jonah is neither a coward nor a cad. The lesson he must learn is in many ways the most difficult lesson of all, theologically and existentially. God calls his prophets not for the purpose of authenticating their prophetic credentials (even when they are authentic) but rather to save others from destruction, even if need be at great cost to the persons and credentials of the prophets themselves. With that in mind, in place of a conclusion, I cite again the one whom Christians confess to be the Clue of clues: "An evil and adulterous generation asks for a sign, but no sign will be given to it except the sign of the prophet Jonah" (Matt 12:39).

Afterword

The germ of this chapter was planted during a three-year consultation on Scriptural Reasoning sponsored by the Center of Theological Inquiry in Princeton, New Jersey. During a long coffee break one morning, several participants and I—Jews, Christians, and Muslims—got into a lively discussion about the relation between historical events and theological truth. My Muslim colleague Mehdi was expressing his puzzlement that Christians could not agree with him that the most important thing about any religion was its message, not the messenger who conveyed it. Kevin and I, the Christians in the group, were fumbling to respond. After a few false starts, I said something to the effect that the message of love must be embodied, or it is not credible. Mehdi was clearly unconvinced. "We Muslims know about love, too," he said.

By the time our conversation ended an hour or so later, we still did not agree about the relation of history and religious truth. But I remember thinking I understood the differences between Christianity and Islam better than I ever had before. The idea of using the book of Jonah came to me then. Previously, it had occurred to me to read it as a kind of allegory of the relationship of Judaism and Christianity. But the idea that the story could be extended to include Islam was new to me. Mehdi helped me to see the story's depiction of the Ninevites in a completely new light. The Ninevites repent because of the message and not the messenger. In this respect, the Ninevites' repentance is very "Muslim," and very different from that of the sailors, for whom dramatic events centering on Jonah play a decisive role.

As I drafted and redrafted my thought experiment, it was important to me that my Jewish and Muslim colleagues be able to see something of their traditions in my interpretation of Jonah. Every time I presented the paper, I tried to improve the portraits a little using the feedback I received. Still, I knew that Jews and Muslims would not be able to endorse everything I said. For example, my Muslim colleague Maria objected to my suggestion that the king of Nineveh was dependent on Jonah, at least insofar as this implied Muhammed's dependence on prior biblical tradition for receiving and communicating the Qur'an. I was grateful to Maria for her objection because it helped clarify where Muslim self-understanding could not see itself in my parable. In the end, however, I decided to leave that detail unchanged. Doing so, it seemed to me, was truer to the book of Jonah. Just as important, it helped preserve the essay's character as an exercise in Christian theology. The experience of doing theology in my tradition in the company of Jews and Muslims doing theology in their traditions was one of the most precious gifts of the three-year project.

9

CHRISTIANITY AND THE POWERS

"GO TELL PHARAOH": OR WHY
EMPIRES PREFER A NAMELESS GOD

At a crucial moment in the book of Exodus, Pharaoh asks Moses, "Who is the Lord, that I should heed him and let Israel go? I do not know the Lord, and I will not let Israel go" (Exod 5:2). Shortly thereafter, God promises—or, perhaps more accurately, threatens—that "you shall know that I am the Lord" (7:17; 8:22; 9:30; etc.). God's promise/threat quickly becomes the golden thread that runs through the rest of the Bible, which repeatedly tells how one day not only Pharaoh and Israel but all creation will acknowledge "that the Lord . . . is God" (Deut 7:9; Josh 4:24; 1 Sam 17:46; Ps 46:10; Ps 100:3; Isa 11:6–9; Hab 2:14; etc.).

The force of Pharaoh's outburst is hidden from us to some degree by the (honorable) conventions of Bible translators. We must remember that what English Bibles typically render as Lord is a Hebrew proper name, *God's* proper name, the Tetragrammaton. When Pharaoh scoffs, "I do not know the Lord," his words have the same force as those of, say, a corporate CEO who has been told that there is a stranger, identified only by name, in the outer office who is just now demanding the company's assets. Pharaoh's reaction is predictable, but the story's outcome is not. What came out of the exodus was a formerly enslaved people that knew its liberated existence to be tied up with God's name and with the practice of taking it seriously (cf. Exod 20:7). It is this very same God and this very same name that Mary celebrates when she sings, "My soul magnifies the Lord. . . . Holy is his name. . . . He has brought down the powerful from their thrones, and lifted up the lowly; he has filled the hungry with good things, and sent the rich away empty" (Luke 1:46, 49, 52–53).

Over time, the people of Israel came to signal respect for God's proper name by ceasing to pronounce it in daily life. That is the custom Mary observes in the passage above. When the Hebrew Bible was translated into Greek, the Tetragrammaton was rendered by the common noun *kyrios*, meaning Lord, and this practice has been followed by most translators of the Bible down to the present day. Even today, Jews do not pronounce God's holy Name, preferring to use some circumlocution in its place such as "The Holy One, Blessed be He" or "Ha'Shem," which simply means "the Name." The practice serves as a perpetual reminder that God's identity and God's mystery are two aspects of the same thing. The God who got Israel out of Egypt is not a nameless *X* but the ineffably mysterious God who revealed God's name to Moses at the burning bush and whose angel spoke to Mary in the hill country of Judaea.

Now, it is just here that the ancient claim of Jewish faith runs directly counter to a deep-seated intuition shared by many people today. It is all well and good, so the sentiment goes, for an ancient people to have believed that God had a personal proper name and chose to reveal it to them as a token of divine favor. But however understandable in its day, this belief has outlived its plausibility and legitimacy. Today it is necessary to see whatever name is most precious to this or that human community against a backdrop of transcendent mystery that exceeds and relativizes all such names. Today human beings need an approach to the transcendent that will provide an effective basis for human solidarity in a shrinking world. Unless we are willing to sacrifice our sacred proper names on the shrine of a greater mystery, how shall we ever find the common spiritual values that we need to end the war of ideologies and give global cooperation a fighting chance?

Several decades ago, the intuition I am describing was defended with great intellectual seriousness in a collection of essays entitled *The Myth of Christian Uniqueness: Toward a Pluralistic Theology of Religions.*[1] While the authors were not of one mind about what a "pluralist theology of religions" would look like, a common theme many stressed was the absolute ineffability of the transcendent referent of all the world's religions. Different religious traditions point toward a reality that is utterly indescribable in itself. In the words of the Indian theologian S. J. Samartha, the "transcendent Center . . . remains always beyond and greater than apprehensions of it or even the sum total of such apprehensions."[2] Behind and beyond the Jew's Lord, the Muslim's Allah, the Hindu's Brahman, and the Christian's Jesus, there lies a reality ineffable in itself that appears under various guises in these tradition-specific names.[3] One author quotes with appreciation a verse from Hindu scripture: "Thou art formless. Thy only form is our knowledge of Thee." For this author, it follows that there is no such thing as idolatry in the traditionally pejorative sense, since all religious concepts are "idols"—that is, human constructs. What is worthy of condemnation is not idolatry as traditionally understood but the hubris of those who identify their own tradition's conception of God with ultimate reality. As the author states, "For Christians to think that Christianity is true, or final, or salvific, is a form of idolatry."[4]

The research program announced by *The Myth of Christian Uniqueness* has since fallen out of favor in academic circles. A more common approach among those who pursue the theological study of religious pluralism today is comparative theology, which seeks to understand the truth of one's "home" religious tradition by comparing it with some other single tradition in a detailed and sympathetic way.[5] But if the message of *The Myth of Christian Uniqueness* no longer resonates in the academy, the same cannot be said for its place in society at large. My experience in the classroom over twenty-five years suggests that students today find the idea of an unknowable God more attractive and plausible than ever. This is true not only for those who do not strongly identify with any religious tradition but also among many who consider themselves to be devoutly Christian. The nameless God may have dropped out of the PhD program, but it seems to be doing very well in seminary and on Main Street.

In one sense, this is hardly surprising. As the authors of *The Myth of Christian Uniqueness* themselves point out, the idea that ultimate reality is strictly ineffable is one of the oldest and most widely attested theological views on record. The ancient Chinese text *Tao Te Ching* begins by affirming "the Tao that can be expressed is not the eternal Tao."[6] The view was also well known to ancient Israel's neighbors the Egyptians. A hymn from an ancient Egyptian papyrus reads, "The One and only, who hides himself from men and gods. No one knows his being. He is higher than the heaven and deeper than the netherworld. No God knows his true appearance. . . . He is too mysterious, one cannot reveal his glory, he is too great that one can search him out, and too powerful to be known."[7] Perhaps it was this very One "who hides himself from men and gods" that Pharaoh had in mind when he asked with outraged incredulity, "Who is the LORD, that I should heed him and let Israel go?" (Exod 5:2).

Yet granted its perennial popularity, we may still wonder why the stock of the nameless God is rising today. In fairness, I think we should admit that the human spirit has been drawn to speak this way for many reasons, including awe and humility before the depthless mystery of life. The authors of *The Myth of Christian Uniqueness* reasonably suggest, too, that many people find it plausible today because they are living in ever-closer proximity to people of other faiths. In addition to these considerations, however, I think we must consider a third and more troubling possibility. The cult of the ineffable God is on the advance because it is politically useful for the consolidation of power, and especially imperial power. Edward Gibbon famously observed that in the age of the Caesars, all religions were "considered by the people equally true, by the philosophers equally false, and by the magistrates equally useful."[8] Gibbon's remark is so amusing it is easy to miss its diagnostic value. The idea that ultimate reality is unknowable is convenient for empires because they seek to unite many disparate peoples, cultures, and religions under a single earthly authority beyond which there is plenty of mystery but no identifiable court of appeal.

It was Alexander the Great who conquered the whole eastern Mediterranean in a few short years and thereby created the political, economic, and cultural conditions that enabled the cult of the unknowable God to attain prominence in the Western world. The court theology that undergirded Alexander's policy and that of his Greek and Latin successors treated different national cults as manifestations of the same deities under different names.[9] This allowed the conquerors to incorporate defeated nations by absorbing their local religions into the larger syncretistic whole of the empire. Today schoolchildren still learn that the Greek *Zeus* and the Roman *Jupiter* were two names for the same god. But as the Dutch antifascist activist and theologian Kornelis Heiko Miskotte wrote in 1941 after his country had been overrun by the Nazis, "The sum total of all the known gods turns out to be, oddly enough, the Unknown."[10] This was exactly the view of antiquity's pagan elites, who commonly maintained that the supreme Deity could in principle have no name. This was different from the Jewish view that the Lord's proper name is not to be *pronounced*. Rather, it held that the supreme Deity was, in the language of middle Platonism, strictly "unnamable and ineffable." God, being beyond comprehension, was also beyond being named, for we can name only what we comprehend. The corollary of this belief was that the nameless Deity could be named in many ways. In the words of the pagan Maximus of Tyre, "We rely on names for the nameless."[11] The theory of the supreme Deity's anonymous polyonomy provided sophisticated pagans with a way to affirm the divine principle of the world independently of exclusive loyalty to the myths, practices, and proper names of this or that local cult. The theory was also attractive to the emperors themselves. Emperor Alexander Severus had in his private chapel not only the statues of the deified emperors but also those of the miracle worker Apollonius of Tyana, Jesus Christ, Abraham, and Orpheus.[12]

Of course, the success of the imperial theology depended on the willingness of the subjugated to identify their own deities with other gods and ultimately with the nameless One. In general, this was not much of an obstacle, for many ancient people were eager to keep their religious portfolios in balance. In the case of the Jews, however, the policy did not work. Alexander's regional successor Antiochus Epiphanes tried to set up the cult of Zeus in the temple in Jerusalem. Following the logic of imperial theology, Zeus and the God who spoke to Moses at the burning bush were simply different manifestations of the same mystery (2 Macc 6:1–2). The Jews didn't see it that way, however, and the incident set off the Maccabean revolt and the eventual repurification of the temple, which is celebrated by Jews today in the festival of Chanukkah. Even such thoroughly hellenized figures as the Jew Philo and the Christian Origen (both residents of the imperial city Alexandria in Egypt) refused to identify the God who spoke to Moses with any of the gods or deities known to the ancient world. When the emperor Caligula decreed that his image should be venerated in the temple in Jerusalem, Philo risked his life by joining a delegation sent to the emperor to protest. A couple of centuries later, the Christian polymath Origen was imprisoned and tortured for his refusal to burn incense to Caesar.

Considering incidents such as these, we can understand why the Greco-Roman world viewed Jews (and later Christians) as atheists. If different cults are simply local manifestations of the same deities, and if these are manifestations of the one supreme being who is nameless and ineffable, then to worship a deity with but one proper name is to abandon God altogether. As we saw, a similar sense of righteous indignation toward traditional Christianity suffuses *The Myth of Christian Uniqueness*, as in the statement that "for Christians to think that Christianity is true, or final, or salvific, is a form of idolatry."[13] Yet here again, I think we need to ask whether a hidden, imperial spirit haunts that proposal, much against the good intentions of the authors themselves. A telling clue in this respect is found in the book's preface, where one of the editors describes the book's common project as "the crossing of a theological Rubicon."[14] As Gavin D'Costa has pointed out, the image is an

ironic one for a research program that claims to seek greater cooperation among the religions. Julius Caesar's original "crossing of
the Rubicon" in 49 BCE was "a forceful attempt to encompass the
'other' within his own framework."[15]

Yet the suspicion I am raising begs an obvious question.
Granted that empires in the past have been undergirded by the
unknowable God, is there an empire today that seeks its blessing?
Isn't it much rather the case that the empires that succeeded ancient
Rome did so in the name of Jesus Christ, the Son of God the Father,
and that the consequences of imperial rule under his name were no
better for Jews and in many cases much worse than under the Caesars? This is true, and it is not a fact that I want to minimize in any
way. Here the warning that "judgment [begins] with the household
of God" (1 Pet 4:17) applies with maximum force. Yet it is also true
that Christian empire's hold on power has steadily eroded since the
dawn of modernity and that today a vastly more powerful successor ideology stands in its place. I am speaking of market rationality,
whose power to bring ever-new domains of life under its control is
being demonstrated at an ever-accelerating pace.

Humans have engaged in market exchange since time imme-
morial. Market exchange permits people to trade commodities
and cash in relative independence of other forces. What distinguishes the modern world is not the existence of markets but their
ever-larger place in the organization of society. In exchange for this
larger space, the market has delivered unprecedented growth in
wealth and standards of living for billions of human beings. But
the growth of the market has not been an unalloyed blessing. As
markets have expanded, they have gradually weakened other
modes of organizing society based on local custom, kinship, religion, and social bond. From the point of view of the market, these
older forms of relation are often inefficient—that is, they created
obstacles to the free exchange of goods and the accumulation of
wealth. Market growth demands that these relationships be dissolved and reshaped in a more rational way—that is, ways that
serve and respond to the demands of the marketplace. Over time,

the growth of the market society has helped shape a new kind of person, a new *I*. Since the economic world is one of constant innovation and flux, the new individuated person is supposed to be free of constraints, unrestricted in its inward life by any bonds to external authority. In the words of Charles Taylor, the new self is "not to identify with any of the tendencies he finds in himself, which can only be the deposits of tradition and authority, but [must] be ready to break and remake these habitual responses according to his own goals." The result is the construction of the *I* as a pure unencumbered self, existing independent of relationships and ready to act for the sake of greater material reward.[16]

It is against this backdrop, I think, that we should understand the rising stock of the cult of the nameless God. Consider three ways in which the nameless God as understood by *The Myth of Christian Uniqueness* reflects and underwrites the logic of the marketplace. In the first place, it transforms diverse religious traditions—each with its unique theology, social formations, and claims to truth—into interchangeable paths or vehicles to the same end. In effect, it repackages them as spiritual commodities which may differ in advertising but which are in substance all offering the same product. Second, it makes the goal of the religious pilgrimage an ineffable, unknown *X* that transcends the names and faces traditionally held sacred by the religions and siphons off their numinous power. Here the analogy to market rationality is especially eerie, for the market too spins around a center that is itself utterly "formless"—namely, capital accumulation. Like the Unknown that results from the mixture of all the gods, the black hole around which the market spins is not wealth in any particular form but wealth as such, which may temporarily manifest itself as dollars, yen, or stock but which has no lasting form in itself and disappears invisibly behind them all. Finally, the nameless God refashions human beings in the image and likeness of itself, as pure unencumbered selves whose own deepest identities are nameless *X*'s that await packaging and marketing for a world where the customer is said to be king but where power in fact resides in the anonymous imperium that rules from above in remote inaccessibility and cold indifference to its subjects.

In all these ways, the cult of the nameless God provides a "sacred canopy" that offers a plausibility structure for market rationality and that underwrites its role as the organizing principle of society and its expansion into ever-new domains of life. Like empires throughout history, market society promises benefits to its multitude of subjects and delivers on these promises in tangible ways. (I am writing this chapter on a laptop that I purchased in a big-box store and that was assembled by low-wage workers in a factory half a world away.) But it also resembles previous empires by taxing its subjects at an exorbitant rate. The market imperium's currency of taxation is the progressive commodification of human life. To take just one looming example, as genetic knowledge becomes completer and more available to consumers through law, prospective parents will be increasingly subject to market pressure to screen their pregnancies for inefficiencies such as mental retardation, genetic disorders, and so on. In time, birth may be reserved for those whose positive genetic traits are deemed to confer a life-long competitive advantage. In such a world, growth to adulthood will entail the discovery that one's very existence has long since been mortgaged to the demands of the marketplace.[17]

I am confident that pockets of resistance of greater and lesser size will challenge the hegemony of market rationality and embody forms of human community that resist the commodification of human life. But I think it unlikely that successful pockets of resistance will form around the shrine of the unknowable God. Empires like having the Unknowable as ultimate principal both because it domesticates the lesser gods and because it is unable to subject the empire itself to radical interrogation. For this reason too, I think it also unlikely that successful pockets of resistance will form around Christian communities that think that the God and Father of Jesus Christ is a provincial outpost of the unknowable God. (I suspect that one reason that Christianity has been vulnerable to imperial capture in the past is that its conception of the

Fatherhood of God has been flawed in this way.) Rather, I think that Christian communities that successfully resist the encroachment of market rationality will take their bearings from the same place that their Jewish siblings have in ages past: the God who entrusted God's personal proper name to Moses at the burning bush.

In this connection, I believe that indispensable significance attaches to the special character of the name that God revealed in the desert on the eve of the exodus and that Mary celebrated in song in the Judaean backcountry. The Tetragrammaton scrambles our ordinary intuitions about the relationship of divine mystery and divine identity. The authors of *The Myth of Christian Uniqueness* are not alone in thinking that the more identifiable God becomes, the more God's mystery is circumscribed and subject to human control. It is this assumption that leads them to define God's mystery as God's unknowable transcendence. But the God who bears the Tetragrammaton is mysteriously uncircumscribable and reliably identifiable at once. Moreover, the two dimensions of God's reality are signified by one and the same sign: the Tetragrammaton itself. Exodus 3 signals this by narrating God's revelation of the Tetragrammaton as a three-step process that begins with God's declaration of two anticipatory names that elucidate the Tetragrammaton in advance from different angles (vv. 14–15). Contrary to what is often supposed, the first of these—"I am who I am"—does not gesture *away* from the Tetragrammaton to a transcendent depth where God is really God in mysterious anonymity, at a safe remove from the Tetragrammaton that God will shortly give to Moses to announce to the Israelites in bondage. Rather, it gestures *toward* the Tetragrammaton and interprets it in advance as the sign of the eternal depths of mystery and uncircumscribability that inhere in God as the bearer of this name. The second elucidating name—"I am has sent me to you" (Exod 3:14)—also gestures toward the Tetragrammaton and assures Israel that the One who bears this name will be present among them as the reliably identifiable God that no one can get a handle on.[18]

The sheer unknowability that *The Myth of Christian Uniqueness* celebrated and that many of my students find attractive is actually a prison beyond which God cannot move. More accurately, it is a sanctuary where putative deity can take refuge without having its credentials called into question. The Bible portrays God's mystery differently. The mystery of God is that God can be reliably identified as the endless mystery that God is. That is the eternal "meaning" of the Tetragrammaton. What this eternal meaning means in time is expounded by the empire-cracking events of Israel's exodus from bondage in Egypt and Jesus of Nazareth's resurrection from the dead.

Human beings are created in order that they may become ever more fully alive as they live into the liberating glory of this God (Irenaeus). They are equipped for this purpose by being creatures who likewise bear personal proper names, public tokens of the fact that each human being is a finite "image and likeness" of God, a creature who is unsubstitutable and uncircumscribable at once. To have a "name divinely understood" (Kierkegaard) is to be impervious to commodification.[19] Pharaoh knew "the Hebrews" by name and yet sought to reduce them to a nameless mass that produced bricks, to units of productive power (Exod 1). Whatever deity undergirded Pharaoh's reign placed no insuperable obstacle in his path. Similarly, the market imperium expands by encroaching on spheres of life that are defined by the unsubstitutability of personal proper names and by incorporating them into the domain of commodity exchange. The nameless God that presides over the market imperium not only does not check this process but greases the way for it by working in advance to refashion the innermost core of human identity in the image of its own anonymous X.

Pharaoh's plans were interrupted from outside his frame of reference by the voice of Ha'Shem, who reinscribed the proper name "Israel" on a wretched people sinking into anonymity and thereby delivered on the promise that "you shall know that I am the LORD!" The same voice, I believe, can awaken Christian communities to recognize the extent of their enmeshment in the market imperium and steel them to become outposts of resistance. If this is to be so, however, Christians must not suppose that the name of Jesus takes the place of Ha'Shem. Jesus comes "in the name of the Lord"; he does not replace it. Like every child of Eve and Adam, Jesus was endowed before birth with a "name divinely understood." What makes Mary's child the Christ is that he lived out his vocation in a way that was fully transparent to the liberating glory of his Father's name. Raised from the dead, Jesus calls his followers by name and thereby incorporates them into a community where they can begin to do the same.

If God is the nameless X that stands equidistant behind and above the world's gods, then the empires of this world are safe. They may struggle for supremacy with one another, but they need not fear a fundamental challenge from beyond. For the unknowable God is infinitely malleable, readily adaptable to the needs of the ruler and hence ultimately unreliable from the perspective of those who are enslaved and perishing. But if God is the One who spoke to Moses from the burning bush, then the empires of this world are shaken at their foundations. For the One who declares "you shall know that I am the Lord!" refuses to become anyone's possession and refuses to countenance the commodification of God's creatures. Blessed be the name of the Lord.

NOTES

Chapter 1: Scripture

1 See Franklin Sherman, *Bridges: Documents of the Christian-Jewish Dialogue*, 2 vols. (Mahwah, NJ: Paulist, 2011, 2014). The International Council of Christians and Jews maintains a current collection of relevant statements on its website. See "Statements," Jewish-Christian Relations: Insights and Issues in the ongoing Jewish-Christian Dialogue, accessed February 1, 2022, https://www.jcrelations.net/statements.html.

2 I think this definition of supersession improves on ones I have given previously by mirroring more closely what I take to be Christian theology's standard procedure when reasoning about teaching errors. (To be clear, I am not claiming that supersessionism is a heresy in a formal sense, only that it is helpful to think about it on analogy with teachings that have been identified as heresies.) In the case of modalism, for example, the chain of reasoning begins with the teaching that the church affirms (i.e., the eternal distinction of the Trinitarian persons), and the error of modalism is defined with reference to it (i.e., the denial of their eternal distinction). The rationales adduced in support of modalism are a distinct sphere of analysis and are examined according to whether or not they necessarily entail modalism (e.g., Jesus said, "I and the Father are one" [John 10:30 NIV]; the Father died on the cross; etc.). Similarly, in the case of supersessionism, I advocate (1) making the affirmation of God's irrevocable election of the Jewish people the logically antecedent reference point for defining supersessionism, (2) defining supersessionism as the contradiction of that affirmation, and (3) making the rationales adduced in support of supersessionism a distinct area of analysis. Here I follow what I understand to be Gavin D'Costa's account of the procedure of the Roman Catholic Church with respect to supersessionism in *Catholic Doctrines on Jews since the Second Vatican Council* (Oxford: Oxford University Press, 2019). I am grateful to Benjamin Preston's unpublished paper "Supersessionism and Post-supersessionist Theology" for helping me to see the importance of approaching the definition of supersessionism in this way. (Elsewhere, I have defined supersessionism in ways that coincide materially with the present definition but that fail to make it as clear that the definition's starting point is the affirmation of God's irrevocable election

of the Jewish people. See *Encyclopedia of Jewish-Christian Relations*, ed. Walter Homolka et al. [Berlin: de Gruyter, 2019], s.v. "supersessionism"; and *A Dictionary of Jewish-Christian Relations*, ed. Edward Kessler and Neil Wenborn [Cambridge: Cambridge University Press, 2005], s.v. "supersessionism.")

Several implications flow from this approach to defining supersessionism that I think are useful for having productive conversation, even between Christians who disagree about whether God has in fact elected the Jewish people irrevocably, and hence whether supersessionism is in fact an error:

1. The definition de-emphasizes the conventional meaning(s) of the word *supersede*. Many academic debates about supersessionism generate more heat than light because they assume that the question turns on the conventional meaning of the word. Debates conducted on this basis quickly become an academic version of a schoolyard squabble ("No, *you're* the one who's being a bully!"). Rather, Christians should use *supersessionism* as a technical term, like *modalism* in the context of Trinitarian theology. It is a more or less arbitrary label for a disputed teaching that can be clearly identified independently of the label itself; other words could be chosen to label the same belief. As a label for the Christian belief that the Jews are not God's elect people, supersessionism has advantages and disadvantages, but so too would any other word chosen for the same purpose (e.g., "replacement theology"). In short, unless people want to argue for a better label (which may well exist), they shouldn't get too hung up on the word itself, and they shouldn't become distracted by what the word means in other contexts.

2. The definition highlights the existence of a logically antecedent ecclesial affirmation with reference to which it is possible to identify supersessionism as an error—in this case, God's irrevocable election of the Jewish people. Importantly, this affirmation can be made the subject of analysis for its own sake without immediate reference to the error that contradicts it. In this respect, it is like the affirmation in relation to which modalism is an error—namely, the eternal distinction of the Trinitarian persons. Bruce D. Marshall, for example, has argued in many places that a necessary corollary of the church's affirmation of God's irrevocable election of the Jewish people is the belief that God forever wills the Jews to exist as a distinct people and that this in turn implies that God wills (in some form) their continued practice of Judaism (see, e.g., Bruce D. Marshall, "Christ and the Cultures: The Jewish People and Christian Theology," in *The Cambridge Companion to Christian Doctrine*, ed. Colin E. Gunton [Cambridge: Cambridge University Press, 1997], 81–100).

I agree with Marshall, but my point at present is the more general one that the concept of supersessionism is dependent on a logically prior affirmation and the necessary implications it entails. In many cases, debates about supersession are unfruitful because they direct attention away from and otherwise skate around this logically prior affirmation and its necessary implications. In short, people who do not think that supersessionism is an error should defend their position by explaining why they think God's election of the Jewish people is not irrevocable.

3. The definition implies that the question of supersessionism should be clearly distinguished from the question of whether Christianity is "truer than" or "superior to" Judaism. David Novak calls the latter belief "soft supersessionism," and he argues that it is a necessary feature of Christian self-understanding, just as the Jewish belief in Judaism's greater truthfulness is obligatory for Jews (see David Novak, "Supersessionism Hard and Soft," *First Things*, February 2019, 290, 27–31). I agree with Novak on the latter point, but I do not think it is helpful to label such beliefs "supersessionism." While I have benefited enormously from Novak's work, I think that his definition of supersessionism risks confusion by using the same term for beliefs that he thinks are obligatory (soft supersessionism) and erroneous (hard supersessionism). Similarly, I do not think that a Christian belief is *necessarily* supersessionist simply because it underwrites the belief that Christianity is "truer than" Judaism (beliefs such as, e.g., that Jesus of Nazareth is the promised Messiah of Israel, that he is the unique and universal Savior of all people, that the new covenant is superior in some respects to the old, etc.). According to the present definition, these beliefs are supersessionist only if they *necessarily* contradict the affirmation that God's election of the Jewish people is irrevocable. While many Christians past and present have supposed that these beliefs do necessarily contradict these affirmations, I do not think that this is so. Of course, the claims are controversial between Christians and Jews, and their truth or falsity may be contested on a variety of grounds. But that question is different from that of whether the beliefs are intrinsically supersessionist. I believe that Christians can affirm the irrevocability of God's election of the Jewish people for the same reasons they think that Christianity rests on God's most complete revelation of God's saving will for humanity.

3 Charles Wood proposed the term "canonical construal" in *The Formation of Christian Understanding: An Essay in Theological Hermeneutics* (Philadelphia: Westminster, 1981), 78. I have proposed speaking instead of a canonical narrative in view of the prominent role played by narrative in the church's traditional canonical construal. See R. Kendall Soulen,

The God of Israel and Christian Theology (Minneapolis: Fortress, 1996), 14. In any case, I regard the terms as interchangeable.

4   Wood, *Christian Understanding*, 109.

5   Irenaeus, *Against Heresies* 1.8.1. On Irenaeus's importance for interpreting the canon as a unity, see Rowan A. Greer, "The Christian Bible and Its Interpretation," in *Early Biblical Interpretation*, ed. James L. Kugel and Rowan A. Greer (Philadelphia: Westminster, 1986), 109–208.

6   Irenaeus, *Against Heresies* 4.9.2.

7   On the rise of historicism and its impact on Christian understandings of the unity of the Bible, see Hans Frei, *The Eclipse of Biblical Narrative* (New Haven, CT: Yale University Press, 1980).

8   Elizabeth Cady Stanton, Susan B. Anthony, and Matilda Josyln Gage, eds., *History of Woman Suffrage*, 4 vols. (New York: Fowler and Wells, 1881; repr., New York: Arno and *New York Times*, 1969), 1:796.

9   For a classic study that makes this case, see Jules Isaac, *Jesus and Israel* (New York: Holt, Rinehart, and Winston, 1971).

10 Elsewhere I have called this feature of the standard canonical narrative "structural supersessionism," but I now think that is an overly broad use of the term *supersessionism* that is best avoided. Israel-forgetfulness is a hermeneutical consequence that frequently flows from the error of supersessionism, but it is not the error itself, nor is supersessionism the only source of Israel-forgetfulness.

11 Soulen, *God of Israel*, x.

12 Lesslie Newbigin, "Missionary Theology in Practice," in *Lesslie Newbigin: Missionary Theologian: A Reader*, comp. Paul Weston (Grand Rapids, MI: Eerdmans, 2006), 138.

13 That is my ambition for the second volume of *The Divine Name(s) and the Holy Trinity* (Louisville, KY: Westminster John Knox, 2011), the first volume of which appeared with the subtitle *Distinguishing the Voices*. Originally, I anticipated that the second volume of *Divine Name(s)* would be limited to the doctrine of God and some case studies, but I gradually realized the project's scope needed to be expanded. The present book is both a second run at the problem I posed in *The God of Israel and Christian Theology* and an "interim report" on the way to the second volume of *Divine Name(s)*.

14 For a fascinating study that examines the Tetragrammaton as the "suppressed memory" of Christianity, see Günter Bader, *Die Emergenz des Namens: Amnesie, Aphasie, Theologie* (Tübingen: Mohr Siebeck, 2006).

Chapter 2: Trinity

1 For influential statements of the two positions, see Elizabeth A. Johnson, *She Who Is: The Mystery of God in Feminist Theological Discourse* (New York: Crossroad, 1993); and Robert W. Jenson, *The Triune Identity: God according to the Gospel* (Philadelphia: Fortress, 1982).

2 For a fuller account of this history, see R. Kendall Soulen, "The Ineffable Name," in *The Oxford Handbook of Apophatic Theology*, ed. John Betz and Rik Van Nieuwenhove (Oxford: Oxford University Press, forthcoming); and Robert J. Wilkinson, *Tetragrammaton: Western Christians and the Hebrew Name of God* (Leiden, Netherlands: Brill, 2015).

3 Martin Luther, Karl Barth, and Robert W. Jenson all advocated this view. See Soulen, *Divine Name(s)*, 61–104.

4 *Oxford English Dictionary*, s.v. "inflection (n.)," accessed February 1, 2022, https://www-oed-com.proxy.library.emory.edu/view/Entry/95497?redirectedFrom=inflection#eid.

5 My labels for the three inflections adopt the "economic" vocabulary of the New Testament rather than that of formal Trinitarian doctrine. My aim is to clearly identify each inflection with the appropriate person while not prejudging the content of the inflections themselves. In one sense, all three inflections are *theological*, since all three concern persons who are equally eternal and divine. The New Testament, however, most commonly uses *theos* to designate the first person of the Trinity, and here I am following New Testament usage. Similarly, *christological* is arguably not a Trinitarian term at all in the strict sense, since it is usually thought not to apply to the eternal identity of the second person distinct from the economy of salvation. Nevertheless, I use it in this context because it clearly picks out the second person of the Trinity. The labels are terms of convenience and are not intended to carry much weight by themselves.

6 I develop the argument of this chapter in greater detail in *Divine Name(s)*.

7 Michael Wyschogrod, *The Body of Faith: God in the People Israel* (San Francisco: Harper & Row, 1989), 91 (italics original).

8 See T. N. D. Mettinger, *In Search of God* (Minneapolis: Fortress, 1987), 8–10.

9 LaCugna, *God for Us: The Trinity and the Christian Life* (New York: HarperCollins, 1991), 302.

10 Kornelis Heiko Miskotte, *Biblical ABCs: The Basics of Christian Resistance*, trans. Eleanora Hof and Collin Cornell (Minneapolis: Fortress, 2021), 54.

11 Moses Maimonides, *Guide for the Perplexed* (Chicago: University of Chicago Press, 1969), 1, 60–62.

12 John Milton, *On the Son of God and the Holy Spirit from His Treatise on Christian Doctrine*, introduction by Alexander Gordon (London: British and Foreign Unitarian Association, 1908), 72 (italics added).

13 On the "divine passive," see Joachim Jeremias, *New Testament Theology: The Proclamation of Jesus* (New York: Scribner's, 1971), 10–14. According to Jeremias, the divine passive occurs about one hundred times in Jesus's sayings.

14 See Sean M. McDonough, *YHWH at Patmos: Rev. 1:4 in Its Hellenistic and Early Jewish Setting* (Tübingen: Mohr Siebeck, 1999), chap. 2.

15 See Carl Judson Davis, *The Name and Way of the Lord: Old Testament Themes, New Testament Christology* (Sheffield, UK: Sheffield Academic, 1996), 93.

16 For discussion and literature, see McDonough, *YHWH at Patmos*, 202–31.

17 See Richard Bauckham, *The Theology of the Book of Revelation* (Cambridge: Cambridge University Press, 1993).

18 Mary McClintock Fulkerson, "Grace, Christian Controversy and Tolerable Falsehoods," in *Grace upon Grace: Essays in Honor of Thomas A. Langford*, ed. Thomas A. Langford et al. (Nashville: Abingdon, 1999), 234.

19 At least one major contributor to the debate has found the thesis advanced here to be sufficiently persuasive to adopt for her own purposes. See Elizabeth A. Johnson, *Quest for the Living God: Mapping Frontiers in the Theology of God* (London: Continuum, 2011), 215–17.

20 Cf. World Council of Churches, *Baptism, Eucharist, and Ministry*, Faith and Order paper no. 111 (Geneva: WCC, 1982), 6.

21 Janet Soskice, *The Kindness of God: Metaphor, Gender, and Religious Language* (Oxford: Oxford University Press, 2008), 4.

22 Soskice, 4.

23 See H. E. W. Turner, *The Pattern of Christian Truth: A Study of the Relations between Orthodoxy and Heresy in the Early Church* (Eugene, OR: Wipf & Stock, 2004), 154, 158.

24 Raymond E. Brown, *The Gospel of John XIII–XXI* (New York: Doubleday, 1970), 755–56.

25 Dale C. Allison, *The Sermon on the Mount* (New York: Crossroad, 1999), 120–21.

26 J. I. Packer, *Knowing God* (Downers Grove, IL: InterVarsity, 1973), 182–83, cited in Marianne Meye Thompson, *The Promise of the Father: Jesus and God in the New Testament* (Louisville, KY: Westminster John Knox, 2000), 11.

27 Maurice Wiles, "Eternal Generation," in *Working Papers in Doctrine* (London: SCM, 1976), 18–27.

28 For a longer list of triads that overlaps very little with this one, see Soulen, *Divine Name(s)*, 249–50.

Chapter 3: Election

1 Michael Dempsey, ed., *Trinity and Election in Contemporary Theology* (Grand Rapids, MI: Eerdmans, 2011), 1. Dempsey's book provides a balanced overview of the debate.

2 Bruce L. McCormack's seminal statement of his position is "Grace and Being: The Role of God's Gracious Election in Karl Barth's Theological Ontology," in *The Cambridge Companion to Karl Barth*, ed. John Bainbridge Webster (Cambridge: Cambridge University Press, 2000), 92–110. A recent defense of the position is Matthias Gockel, "How to Read Karl Barth with Charity: A Critical Reply to George Hunsinger," *Modern Theology* 32, no. 2 (2016): 259–67.

3 George Hunsinger's fullest statement of his position is found in *Reading Barth with Charity: A Hermeneutical Proposal* (Grand Rapids, MI: Baker, 2015). See also Paul Molnar, *Divine Freedom and the Doctrine of the Immanent Trinity* (London: T&T Clark, 2002).

4 For an overview of modern historical research into the origins and meaning of the Divine Name, see Wilkinson, *Tetragrammaton*, 1–41.

5 The Johannine pattern of thought provides a firm biblical foundation for the Trinitarian tradition's subsequent affirmation of the monarchy of the first person of the Trinity and the teaching known as "essential communication," keystones of the patristic and medieval doctrine of the Trinity in the East and West. See Giles Emery, *The Trinitarian Theology of St. Thomas Aquinas* (Oxford: Oxford University Press, 2007), 156. The eternal giving and receiving of the Divine Name are the biblical original for which "the eternal communication of the divine essence" provides the hellenizing paraphrase. There is nothing wrong with the paraphrase, provided it does not suffer from Tetragrammaton-amnesia, which, unfortunately, it normally does. For an excellent treatment of essential communication, together with John Calvin's idiosyncratic opposition to it, see Brannon Ellis, *Calvin, Classical Trinitarianism, and the Aseity of the Son* (Oxford: Oxford University Press, 2012). While Ellis favors Calvin's critique of the doctrine, his book provides an illuminating and fair-minded overview of the role the idea has played in configuring the doctrine of the Trinity.

6 On the significance of the Tetragrammaton for the Fourth Gospel, see Joshua J. F. Coutts, *The Divine Name in the Gospel of John: Significance and Impetus*, WUNT II (Tübingen: Mohr Siebeck, 2017). See also Richard Bauckham, "Monotheism and Christology in the Gospel of John," in *Contours of Christology in the New Testament*, by Richard N. Longenecker (Grand Rapids, MI: Eerdmans, 2005), 148–66; Charles A. Gieschen, "The

Divine Name in Ante-Nicene Christology," *Vigiliae Christianae* 57, no. 2 (2003): 115–58; and Brown, *The Gospel according to John*, 755–56.

7 See Bauckham, "Monotheism and Christology," 154–63; and Catrin H. Williams, *I Am He: The Interpretation of* "Anî Hû" *in Jewish and Early Christian Literature* (Tübingen: Mohr Siebeck, 2000).

8 Gieschen, "Divine Name," 141.

9 NRSV, translation slightly modified.

10 Karl Barth, *Church Dogmatics*, vol. 2, no. 2, ed. Geoffrey William Bromiley and Thomas Forsyth Torrance, trans. Geoffrey William Bromiley et al. (Edinburgh: T&T Clark, 1975).

11 Barth, *Church Dogmatics*, vol. 2, no. 2, 5, 54, 59, 60, 103, etc.

12 Karl Barth, *Church Dogmatics*, vol. 1, no. 1, ed. Geoffrey William Bromiley and Thomas Forsyth Torrance, trans. Geoffrey William Bromiley (Edinburgh: T&T Clark, 1975), 348.

13 Barth, *Church Dogmatics*, vol. 2, no. 2, 99–106.

14 McCormack, "Grace and Being," 100.

15 Bruce McCormack, "Seek God Where He May Be Found," in *Orthodox and Modern: Studies in the Theology of Karl Barth* (Grand Rapids, MI: Baker Academic, 2008), 274.

16 Karl Barth, *Church Dogmatics*, vol. 1, no. 1, 348.

17 Barth's theology of Israel is too complex to adequately assess here; a fuller account would need to be more appreciative than I am in this chapter. See R. Kendall Soulen, "Karl Barth and the Future of the God of Israel," *Pro Ecclesia* 6, no. 4 (Fall 1997): 413–28. For a variety of contemporary assessments, see George Hunsinger, ed., *Karl Barth: A Post-Holocaust Theologian?* (Grand Rapids, MI: Eerdmans, 2018). In my opinion, the most illuminating systematic study of the issues at stake is Bertold Klappert, *Israel und die Kirche: Erwägungen zur Israellehre Karl Barths* (Munich: Kaiser, 1980).

18 Karl Barth, *Die christliche Dogmatik im Entwurf,* vol. 1, *Die Lehre vom Wrote Gottes: Prolegomena zur christlichen Dogmatik* [1927], ed. Gerhard Sauter, in *Akademische Werke, Gesamtausgabe 2*, by Karl Barth (Zurich: Theologischer, 1982), 233.

19 Barth, *Church Dogmatics*, vol. 1, no. 1, 348.

20 Barth, *Church Dogmatics*, vol. 1, no. 2, 226.

21 Barth, *Church Dogmatics*, vol. 3, no. 2, ed. G. W. Bromiley and T. F. Torrance, trans. G. W. Bromiley (Edinburgh: T&T Clark, 1960), 584 (italics added).

22 Barth, *Church Dogmatics*, vol. 1, no. 1, 318.

23 Barth, 318 (italics original).

Chapter 4: Covenant

1 See, e.g., E. W. Nicholson, *Deuteronomy and Tradition* (Philadelphia: Fortress, 1967), 70; and Bruce K. Walke, *An Old Testament Theology: An Exegetical, Canonical, and Thematic Approach* (Grand Rapids, MI: Zondervan, 2011), 509.

2 David Pawson, *Christianity Explained* (Santa Fe, NM: Terra Nova, 2006), 40.

3 Janice Prager and Arlene Lepoff, *Why Be Different? A Look into Judaism* (Springfield, NJ: Behrman House, 1986), 3.

4 See, e.g., Michael Wyschogrod, "A Theology of Jewish Unity," in *Abraham's Promise: Judaism and Jewish-Christian Relations*, by Michael Wyschogrod, ed. R. Kendall Soulen (Grand Rapids, MI: Eerdmans, 2004), 43–52.

5 David Novak, *Zionism and Judaism: A New Theory* (Cambridge: Cambridge University Press, 2015), 133, 128. God's spontaneous love as the ground of election may be interpreted on analogy with the irrational, erotically charged human experience of "falling in love." Cf. Wyschogrod, *Body of Faith*, 61–64; and Jon D. Levenson, "The Universal Horizon of Biblical Particularism," in *The Bible and Ethnicity*, ed. Mark G. Brett (Leiden, Netherlands: Brill, 1996), 143–69. However, it needn't be. David Novak does not interpret God's electing love for Israel in that way, and it is not the way I would choose to interpret it. In my opinion, the analogy fails to do justice to Barth's insight that the biblically attested God "loves in freedom." It also fails to do justice to the fact that God's love creates the beloved, as I discuss below.

6 See Bruce D. Marshall, "Religion and Election: Aquinas on Natural Law, Judaism, and Salvation in Christ," *Nova et vetera* 14, no. 1 (Winter 2016): 111.

7 Roy Schoeman, "Catholicism and Judaism," in *The Catholic Church and the World Religions: A Theological and Phenomenological Account*, ed. Gavin D'Costa (London: T&T Clark, 2011), 51 (italics added).

8 Joel S. Kaminsky, *Yet I Loved Jacob: Reclaiming the Biblical Concept of Election* (Nashville: Abingdon, 2007), 156.

9 Christopher J. H. Wright, *The Mission of God: Unlocking the Bible's Grand Narrative* (Westmont, IL: IVP Academic, 2006). Henceforth, all page references will be given in parentheses in the text.

10 Richard Bauckham, "Biblical Theology and the Problems of Monotheism," in *Out of Egypt: Biblical Theology and Biblical Interpretation*, ed. Craig Bartholomew, Mary Healy, Karl Möller, and Robin Parry (Milton Keynes: Paternoster, 2004), 210–11.

11 My criticism of C. H. J. Wright's instrumental interpretation of Israel's election is similar to criticism that has been directed at N. T. Wright for the same reasons. See Sigurd Grinkheim, "Election and the Role of Israel," in *God and the Faithfulness of Paul: Critical Examination of the Pauline Theology of N. T. Wright*, WUNT 2/413, ed. Christoph Heilig, J. Thomas Hewitt, and Michael F. Bird (Tübingen: Mohr Siebeck, 2016), 329–46; and Joel Kaminsky and Mark Reasoner, "The Meaning and Telos of Israel's Election: An Interfaith Response to N. T. Wright's Reading of Paul," *Harvard Theological Review* 112, no. 4 (2019): 421–46.

12 Lesslie Newbigin, *The Household of God: Lectures on the Nature of the Church* (Eugene, OR: Wipf & Stock, 2008), 148.

13 C. G. Montefiore and H. Loewe, eds., *A Rabbinic Anthology* (New York: Meridian Books, 1960), 116. Other Jewish authors adopt the definition verbatim or echo it in very similar terms. See Leyla Gurkan, *The Jews as a Chosen People: Tradition and Transformation* (New York: Routledge, 2008), 34; Lavinia Cohn-Sherbok and Dan Cohn-Sherbok, *Medieval Jewish Philosophy: An Introduction* (New York: Routledge, 2014), 19; and Adele Berlin and Marc Zvi Brettler, eds., *The Jewish Study Bible*, 2nd ed. (Oxford: Oxford University Press, 2014), on Leviticus 22:31–33.

14 On the relevance of "YHWH" and "Israel" as proper names for understanding God's covenant with Israel, see David Novak, *The Election of Israel: The Idea of the Chosen People* (Cambridge: Cambridge University Press, 1995), 222.

15 Bauckham, "Biblical Theology," 210–11.

16 Tommy Givens rightly emphasizes the porousness and indefinability of Israel's identity as God's chosen people in *We the People: Israel and the Catholicity of Jesus* (Minneapolis: Fortress, 2014).

17 So, at any rate, God's eternal saving purpose is understood in my own Wesleyan tradition. Of God's saving decree, Charles Wesley wrote, "Thou has all in Christ elected, not a soul of the whole was by Thee rejected." Charles Wesley, *The Poetical Words of John and Charles Wesley*, vol. 3, collected and arranged by G. Osborn (London: Wesleyan-Methodist Conference Office, 1869), 101.

18 Søren Kierkegaard, *The Sickness unto Death: A Christian Psychological Exposition for Upbuilding and Awakening*, ed. and trans. Howard V. Hong and Edna H. Hong (Princeton: Princeton University Press, 1983), 33–34.

19 Kaminsky, *Yet I Loved Jacob*, 156.

20 Michael Wyschogrod, "Incarnation and God's Indwelling in Israel," in Wyschogrod, *Abraham's Promise*, 165–78.

Chapter 5: Christ

1 Augustine of Hippo illustrates the pattern in this statement:

> The sacraments of the Old Testament, which were celebrated in obedience to the law, were types of Christ who was to come; and when Christ fulfilled them by His advent they were done away, and were done away because they were fulfilled. For Christ came not to destroy, but to fulfill. And now that the righteousness of faith is revealed, and the children of God are called into liberty, and the yoke of bondage which was required for a carnal and stiff-necked people is taken away, other sacraments are instituted, greater in efficacy, more beneficial in their use, easier in performance, and fewer in number.

Augustine of Hippo, *Reply to Faustus the Manichaean,* in *St. Augustin: The Writings against the Manichaeans and against the Donatists,* vol. 4, ed. Philip Schaff, trans. R. Stothert (Buffalo, NY: Christian Literature, 1887), 244.

2 Cf. Thomas Aquinas, *Summa theologiae* Ia–IIae, q. 103, a. 4; q. 104, a. 3.

3 Michael Wyschogrod drew attention to the teaching's problematic implications in "A Jewish Reading of Thomas Aquinas on the Old Law," in *Understanding the Scriptures,* ed. C. Thomas and M. Wyschogrod (Mahwah, NJ: Paulist, 1987), 125–38. The nexus of issues is discussed extensively in D'Costa, *Catholic Doctrines;* and Matthew Tapie, *Aquinas on Israel and the Church: The Question of Supersessionism in the Theology of Thomas Aquinas* (Eugene, OR: Pickwick, 2014).

4 My account of the Tetragrammaton in the Second Temple period draws heavily on McDonough's splendid book *YHWH at Patmos.*

5 It is not easy to pin down the precise nomenclature that would appropriately describe this ancient feature of Jewish piety. The practice is so deeply rooted, it is not easily classified. To employ the framework of rabbinic Judaism in its developed form, name avoidance is for first-century Jews (and those of later periods) a matter of "Oral Torah," or universal, authoritative halakah. Indeed, it might be regarded as so self-evident that it would (anachronistically) be seen as a matter of Written rather than Oral Torah. In any case, it would not fall under the category of mere "custom" (*minhag*), a technical legal term in rabbinic thought that refers to observances that are adopted in certain local communities but not in others. On the other hand, historians caution that the notion of Oral Torah in its rabbinic sense did not emerge until later, perhaps the third century CE, and can be applied only with some anachronism to the first-century Jewish world. The Pharisees had "oral traditions," but the use of the singular noun (oral tradition) to refer to a second type of "Torah" (the "dual Torah") is not extant in the first century. Labeled in terms of the threefold categorization of the Mosaic law that became conventional among Christians, the practice belongs to the ceremonial

law rather than the moral or civil law, though Christians have more commonly denounced it as Jewish superstition. On the last point, see Wilkinson, *Tetragrammaton*, 313–415.

6 Julius Boehmer, *Die neutestamenliche Gottesscheu und die ersten drei Bitten des Vaterunsers* (Halle [Saale]: Richard Mühlmann, 1917), 2–3.

7 Despite its age, an excellent overview remains Gustaf Dalman's work *The Words of Jesus Considered in the Light of Post-biblical Jewish Writings and the Aramaic Language*, trans. D. M. Kay (Edinburgh: T&T Clark, 1909). Scholars who have extended this line of research include Joachim Jeremias, Charles A. Gieschen, Martin Hengel, Larry Hurtado, Richard Bauckham, Sean McDonough, C. Kavin Rowe, W. D. Davies, Raymond Brown, Dale C. Allison, Scott McKnight, and Karl Judson Davis.

8 Dalman, *Words of Jesus*, 196, 206 (italics added).

9 NRSV, translation slightly modified.

10 NRSV, translation slightly modified.

11 Dalman, 226–29. The idiosyncratic form of dominical speech is also discussed in Larry Hurtado, *Lord Jesus Christ: Devotion to Jesus in Earliest Christianity* (Grand Rapids, MI: Eerdmans, 2005), 292; and Bruce Chilton, "'Amen': An Approach through Syriac Gospels," in *Targumic Approaches to the Gospels: Essays in the Mutual Definition of Judaism and Christianity* (Lanham, MD: University Press of America, 1986), 15–23.

12 On the "divine passive" in Jesus's speech, see Dalman, *Words of Jesus*, 224–26; Paul Billerbeck and Lermann Strack, *Kommentar zum Neuen Testament aus Talmud und Midrasch*, vol. 1 (Munich: Beck, 1922), 330; and Jeremias, *New Testament Theology*, 9–14.

13 On the Tetragrammaton in the Lord's Prayer, see Jan Muis, *The Implicit Theology of the Lord's Prayer: A Biblical and Theological Investigation*, trans. Allan J. Janssen (Lanham, MD: Lexington/Fortress, 2020), 137–38; Adelheid Ruck-Schroeder, *Der Name Gottes und der Name Jesu* (Neukirchen-Vlyun, Germany: Neukirchener, 1999), 149–50; and Lyder Brun, "Der Name und die Königsherrschaft im Vaterunser," in *Harnack-Ehrung: Beiträge zur Kirchengeschichte zu seinem 70. Geburtstage dargebracht von einer Reihe seiner Schüler* (Leipzig: Hinrichs'sche, 1921), 22–31.

14 On the first petition of the Lord's Prayer as divine passive, see W. D. Davies and Dale C. Allison Jr., *A Critical and Exegetical Commentary on the Gospel according to Saint Matthew*, vol. 1 (Edinburgh: T&T Clark, 1988), 602; and Raymond E. Brown, "The Pater Noster as an Eschatological Prayer," in *New Testament Essays* (Garden City, NY: Doubleday Image, 1968), 319.

15 Elsewhere, the New Testament reports the Father speaking to Jesus or vice versa but not a verbal exchange between them. On the significance

of John 12:28 for the Gospel of John, see Coutts, *Divine Name*, 71–120; and R. Kendall Soulen, "The Father's Voice: Reclaiming a Neglected Aspect of the Doctrine of the Trinity," *Pro Ecclesia* 31, no. 2 (May 2022).

16 Gieschen, "Divine Name," 141.

17 Otto Weber, *Foundations of Dogmatics*, vol. 1, trans. Darrell L. Guder (Grand Rapids, MI: Eerdmans, 1981), 418.

18 See Wilkinson, *Tetragrammaton*, 315–50.

19 Boehmer, *Die ersten drei Bitten*, 210–11.

20 Matthew Levering, "Thomas Aquinas on Law and Love," *Angelicum* 94, no. 2 (2017): 413–41.

21 Congregation for Divine Worship and the Discipline of the Sacraments, *Letter to the Bishop's Conferences on "The Name of God"* (Washington, DC: United States Conference of Catholic Bishops, 2008), 1, https://www.usccb.org/prayer-and-worship/the-mass/frequently-asked-questions/upload/name-of-god.pdf.

22 Congregation for Divine Worship and the Discipline of the Sacraments, *Letter to the Bishop's Conferences*, 1–3.

Chapter 6: Church

1 See, e.g., the World Council of Churches, *The Nature and Mission of the Church: A Stage on the Way to a Common Statement*, Faith and Order paper no. 198 (Geneva: WCC, 1998), and its predecessor statements.

2 Second Vatican Council, *Lumen Gentium: Dogmatic Constitution on the Church*, 9–17, https://www.vatican.va/archive/hist_councils/ii_vatican _council/documents/vat-ii_const_19641121_lumen-gentium_en.html.

3 Robert W. Jenson, *Systematic Theology*, vol. 2, *The Works of God* (Oxford: Oxford University Press, 1999), 191–94. For Jenson's theology of Israel, see also Robert W. Jenson, "Toward a Christian Theology of Israel," *Pro Ecclesia* 9, no. 1 (Winter 2000): 43–56. For studies of Jenson's theology of Israel, see Sang Hoon Lee, *Trinitarian Ontology and Israel in Robert W. Jenson's Theology* (Eugene, OR: Wipf & Stock, 2016); and Andrew W. Nicol, *Exodus and Resurrection: The God of Israel in the Theology of Robert W. Jenson* (Minneapolis: Fortress, 2016).

4 Jenson, *Systematic Theology*, 2:190.

5 Irenaeus of Lyon, *On the Apostolic Preaching*, trans. and introduction by John Behr (Crestwood, NY: St. Vladimir's Seminary Press, 1997), 44.

6 Irenaeus, 44.

7 Second Vatican Council, *Ad Gentes: Decree on the Mission Activity of the Church*, 7, https://www.vatican.va/archive/hist_councils/ii_vatican _council/documents/vat-ii_decree_19651207_ad-gentes_en.html.

8 *The Works of Jonathan Edwards*, vol. 13, *The "Miscellanies," a-500*, ed. Thomas A. Schafer (New Haven, CT: Yale University Press, 1994), 235. My reading of Augustine has been especially assisted by Lewis Ayres, *Augustine and the Trinity* (Cambridge: Cambridge University Press, 2010); and Luigi Gioia, *The Theological Epistemology of Augustine's* De Trinitate (Oxford: Oxford University Press, 2008). On the revelation of the Father as the purpose of the divine missions, see Gioia, *Theological Epistemology*, 106–46; Ayers, *Augustine and the Trinity*, 181–88; and Emmanuel Durand, "God the Father," in *The Oxford Handbook of the Trinity*, ed. Giles Emery and Mathew Levering (Oxford: Oxford University Press, 2011), 371–86. In contrast to Augustine, Robert Jenson most commonly describes the narrative logic of salvation history as running *a Patri ad Spiritus*. On this point, I side with Augustine. For a systematic theology in a Jensonian spirit that emphatically moves *a Patri ad Patrem*, see Paul Hinlicky, *The Beloved Community: Critical Dogmatics after Christendom* (Grand Rapids, MI: Eerdmans, 2015).

9 Miskotte, *Biblical ABCs*, 32.

10 On "Alpha and Omega" as a surrogate for the Divine Name, see McDonough, *YHWH at Patmos*, 200, 217–20.

11 See Klappert, *Israel und die Kirche*.

12 Yehezekel Landau et al., eds., *John Paul II in the Holy Land—in His Own Words* (Mahwah, NJ: Paulist, 2005), 121.

13 "The Gifts and the Calling of God Are Irrevocable: A Reflection on Theological Questions Pertaining to Catholic-Jewish Relations on the Occasion of the 50th Anniversary of 'Nostra Aetate' (No. 4)," Commission for Religious Relations with the Jews, para. 43, accessed February 2022, http://www.christianunity.va/content/unitacristiani/en/commissione-per-i-rapporti-religiosi-con-l-ebraismo/commissione-per-i-rapporti-religiosi-con-l-ebraismo-crre/documenti-della-commissione/en.html.

14 Barth, *Church Dogmatics*, vol. 2, no. 2, 206–10.

15 Levering, "Thomas Aquinas."

16 On the antiphonal pattern of "call and response" as a distinctively African and African American mode of praise and cultural production, see Patricia Liggins Hill, ed., *Call and Response: The Riverside Anthology of the African American Literary Tradition* (Boston: Houghton Mifflin, 1997). On the importance of Black worship traditions for the health of the whole church, see Richard N. Soulen, "Black Worship and Hermeneutic," *Christian Century*, February 11, 1970, 168–71.

17 See Edmund Hill's introductory essay to Augustine, *The Trinity*, 2nd ed., introduction, trans., and notes by Edmund Hill (New York: New City, 1991), 51–52. Citations of Augustine are from this edition.

18 Augustine, *Trinity*, 97–126.

19 Irenaeus of Lyon, *Irenaeus against Heresies*, in *The Apostolic Fathers with Justin Martyr and Irenaeus*, vol. 1, ed. A. Roberts, J. Donaldson, and A. C. Coxe (Buffalo, NY: Christian Literature, 1885), 5.16.1.

20 In fairness to Augustine, he recognizes that the Father speaks in the new covenant, and he even accords "the Father's voice" a prominent place in his summary of Catholic faith about the Trinity (*Trinity*, 70–71). The curious thing is that Augustine's probing mind leaves this feature of the church's faith almost completely undeveloped in his reflections on how the Trinity is revealed in the economy of salvation (with the exception of wondering about how the Father's voice was made audible), prompting the subsequent tradition that built on Augustine to largely overlook the Father's voice as well. In contrast, Robert Jenson emphasizes the importance of the Father's voice as a canon-unifying theme in his *Systematic Theology*. On the importance of the Father's voice for understanding the Father's unique hypostatic identity, see Soulen, "Father's Voice." On the importance of the Father's voice for the genesis of Trinitarian thought, see the recent studies on "prosoponic exegesis" in the New Testament in Matthew Bates, *The Hermeneutics of Apostolic Proclamation: The Center of Paul's Method of Scriptural Interpretation* (Waco, TX: Baylor University Press, 2019); and Matthew Bates, *The Birth of the Trinity: Jesus, God, and Spirit in New Testament and Early Christian Interpretation of the Old Testament* (Oxford: Oxford University Press, 2016).

21 Augustine, *Trinity*, 183.

22 Augustine, 183.

23 See Richard Bauckham, "James and the Gentiles (Acts 15.13–21)," in *History, Literature and Society in the Book of Acts*, ed. Ben Witherington III (Cambridge: Cambridge University Press, 1996), 154–84.

24 For a discussion of problems with the exegetical tradition of Old Testament christophanies, see Fred Sanders, *The Triune God* (Grand Rapids, MI: Zondervan, 2016), chap. 8.

25 Thompson, *Promise of the Father*; Ben Witherington III and Laura M. Ice, *The Shadow of the Almighty: Father, Son, and Holy Spirit in Biblical Perspective* (Grand Rapids, MI: Eerdmans, 2002).

26 Linn Tonstad has argued persuasively that it is an error to import gendered construals of human personhood into the divine life. With Janet Soskice, however, I would maintain that the primary concern of the Bible's use of gendered language for God is kinship rather than gender or sexual difference per se (Soskice, *Kindness of God*). It seems to me that the Fourth Gospel in particular invites us to understand divine kinship

as nongendered in light of the Word/Son/Name-Receiver's nongendered relation to God/Father/Name-Giver. Divine kinship in Christ funds, reorders, and chastens human kinship in a way that deprives its gendered expression of transcendent foundation. Tonstad also argues that traditional accounts of the Trinitarian relations of origin suffer from an overemphasis on the vocabulary of divine kinship. I agree wholeheartedly. However, I think the best remedy is not to drop the relations of origin, which are too deeply rooted in the biblical witness to jettison, but rather to break the monopoly of kinship vocabulary for our understanding of them. See Linn Tonstad, *God and Difference: The Trinity, Sexuality, and the Transformation of Finitude* (New York: Routledge, 2016).

27 For recent exegetical studies that draw attention to this dimension of the NT, see Mark Nanos and Magnus Zetterholm, eds., *Paul within Judaism: Restoring the First-Century Context to the Apostle* (Philadelphia: Fortress, 2015); Caroline E. Johnson Hodge, *If Sons, Then Heirs: A Study of Kinship and Ethnicity in the Letters of Paul* (Oxford: Oxford University Press, 2007); and Paula Fredriksen, "Why Should a 'Law-Free' Mission Mean a 'Law-Free' Apostle?," *Journal of Biblical Literature* 134, no. 3 (2015): 637–50.

28 Barth, *Church Dogmatics*, vol. 2, no. 2, 206–10.

29 See Carolinne White, *The Correspondence (394–419), between Jerome and Augustine of Hippo* (Lewiston, NY: E. Mellen, 1990), 2–3, 43–47, 120–32. See also Daniel Boyarin, *Border Lines: The Partition of Judaeo-Christianity* (Philadelphia: University of Pennsylvania Press, 2006), 209; and Peter J. Gorday, "Jews and Gentiles, Galatians 2:11–14, and Reading Israel in Romans: The Patristic Debate," in *Engaging Augustine on Romans: Self, Context, and Theology in Interpretation*, ed. Daniel Patte and Eugene TeSelle (Harrisburg, PA: Continuum International, 2002), 199–236.

30 See J. Kameron Carter, *Race: A Theological Account* (New York: Oxford University Press, 2008); and Willie James Jennings, *The Christian Imagination: Theology and the Origins of Race* (New Haven, CT: Yale University Press, 2010). For a fine-grained historical account of how supersessionism is intertwined with the ideology of white supremacy in the twentieth century, see Michael Barkun, *Religion and the Racist Right: The Origins of the Christian Identity Movement* (Chapel Hill: University of North Carolina Press, 1997).

31 Jennings, *Christian Imagination*, 275.

32 Jenson, *Systematic Theology*, 2:222.

Chapter 7: Christians and Jews

1 See Sherman, *Bridges*. The International Council of Christians and Jews maintains a current collection of such statements on its website. See "Statements."

2 The literature on Romans 9–11 is vast beyond review. For a recent overview with extensive bibliography, see Florian Wilk and J. Ross Wagner, eds., *Between Gospel and Election: Explorations in the Interpretation of Romans 9–11* (Tübingen: Mohr Siebeck, 2010). This chapter is a revised version of an essay that appeared in that volume. See also Todd D. Still, *God and Israel: Providence and Purpose in Romans 9–11* (Waco, TX: Baylor University Press, 2017).

3 Daniel B. Wallace, *Greek Grammar beyond the Basics: An Exegetical Syntax of the New Testament with Scripture, Subject, and Greek Word Indexes* (Grand Rapids, MI: Zondervan, 1997), 521. See J. Brian Tucker, *Readings Romans after Supersessionism* (Eugene, OR: Cascade, 2018), 124.

4 Lewis Carroll, *Alice's Adventures in Wonderland and Through the Looking Glass* (London: Reader's Library, 2021), 178.

5 Bertold Klappert, "Traktat für Israel (Römer 9–11): Die paulinsiche Verhaeltnisbestiummung von Israel und die Kirche als Kriterium neutestamentlicher Sachaussagen über die Juden," in *Jüdische Existenz und die Erneuerung der christlichen Theologie*, ed. Martin Stöhr (Munich: Christian Kaiser, 1981), 85. See also Klappert's collection of essays, *Miterben der Verheissung: Beiträge zum jüdisch-christlichen Dialog* (Neukirchen-Vluyn, Germany: Neukirchener, 2000).

6 Though I do not subscribe to all its conclusions, a penetrating study of this point is Hans Hübner, *Gottes Ich und Israel: Zum Schriftgebrauch des Paulus in Römer 9–11* (Göttingen: Vandenhoeck & Ruprecht, 1984).

7 The divine "first person" in Romans 9–11. First-person verbal conjugations: 9:9 (1×), 13 (2×), 15 (4×), 17 (1×), 25 (2×), 33 (1×); 10:19 (1×), 20 (2×), 21 (1×); 11:4 (1×), 27 (1×). Pronouns such as *ego, mou, eme*, and so on: 9:17 (2×), 25 (2×), 26 (1×); 10:17 (1×), 20 (2×), 21 (1×); 11:27 (1×).

8 Important works that develop this last point are Mark Kinzer, *Searching Her Own Mystery: Nostra Aetate, the Jewish People, and the Identity of the Church* (Eugene, OR: Cascade 2015); Gavin D'Costa, *Catholic Doctrines on Jews since the Second Vatican Council* (Oxford: Oxford University Press, 2019).

Chapter 8: Christianity, Judaism, and Islam

1 Jon Levenson, "The Conversion of Abraham to Judaism, Christianity, and Islam," in *The Idea of Biblical Interpretation: Essays in Honor of James L.*

Kugel, ed. Hindy Najman and Judith H. Newman (Leiden, Netherlands: Brill, 2004), 3–40.

2 Martin S. Jaffee advances the thesis that "Judaism, Christianity, and Islam are equally rich, historical embodiments of a single structure of discourse that underlies the historically developed symbol systems specific to each community," and maintains that this fact accounts the way "monotheistic communities distinguish themselves from other such communities." Martin S. Jaffee, "One God, One Revelation," *Journal of the American Academy of Religion* 69, no. 4 (December 2001): 753–75, 757.

3 On the different shapes that supersessionism may take in the Jewish tradition, see Novak, "Supersessionism."

4 Although the Qur'an explicitly speaks of the Torah and the Gospels as divine revelations, Muslims do not consider the Old and New Testaments in their current form to be sacred writings.

5 On typology in early Christian tradition, see John J. O'Keefe and R. R. Reno, *Sanctified Vision: An Introduction to Early Christian Interpretation of the Bible* (Baltimore: Johns Hopkins University Press, 2005). For typology in the Hebrew Bible, see Michael Fishbane, *Biblical Interpretation in Ancient Israel* (Oxford: Clarendon, 1985). Other classic studies include Erich Auerbach, "Figura," in *Scenes from the Drama of European Literature* (Gloucester, MA: Peter Smith, 1973), 11–76; and James S. Preus, *From Shadow to Promise: Old Testament Interpretation from Augustine to the Young Luther* (Cambridge, MA: Harvard University Press, 1969).

6 Irenaeus, *Against Heresies*, bk. 3.20, in *Ante-Nicene Fathers*, ed. Alexander Roberts and James Donaldson, vol. 1 (Peabody, MA: Hendrickson, 2004), 449.

7 Augustine, *Letter* 102, in *Nicene and Post-Nicene Fathers*, ed. Philip Schaff, ser. 1, vol. 2 (Peabody, MA: Hendrickson, 2004), 424.

8 Augustine, 2:424.

9 Augustine, 2:424.

10 Augustine, 2:425. Translation altered slightly for clarity.

11 Quotations from the book of Jonah come from the NRSV, unless otherwise indicated. The NRSV renders the name YHWH with "the Lord," but I have substituted the unvocalized Name to make the author's name theology more clearly visible.

12 Arabic and Hebrew are both Semitic languages and have much in common. The Arabic word for a god is *ilah* and is related to the Hebrew *el*, from which *elohim* is also derived. The name "Allah" is probably the word *ilah* combined with the definite article, meaning "the God"—that is, "the one and only God."

Chapter 9: Christianity and the Powers

1 John Hick and Paul F. Knitter, eds., *The Myth of Christian Uniqueness: Toward a Pluralistic Theology of Religions* (Maryknoll, NY: Orbis, 1987).

2 S. J. Samartha, "The Cross and the Rainbow: Christ in a Multireligious Culture," in Hick and Knitter, *Myth of Christian Uniqueness*, 75.

3 J. A. DiNoia, "Pluralist Theology of Religions: Pluralistic or Non-Pluralistic," in *Christian Uniqueness Reconsidered: The Myth of a Pluralistic Theology of Religions*, ed. Gavin D'Costa (Maryknoll, NY: Orbis, 1990), 129.

4 Wilfred Cantwell Smith, "Idolatry: In Comparative Perspective," in Hick and Knitter, *Myth of Christian Uniqueness*, 56.

5 See Francis X. Clooney, *Comparative Theology: Deep Learning across Religious Borders* (Chichester, UK: Wiley-Blackwell, 2010); and Francis X. Clooney, ed., *The New Comparative Theology: Interreligious Insights from the Next Generation* (London: T&T Clark International, 2010).

6 Lao Tzu, *The Sayings of Lao Tzu*, trans. Lionel Giles (Knutsford, UK: A&D, 2008), 5.

7 Peter Gerlitz, "Name/Namengebung I," in *Theologische Realenzyklopädie*, vol. 23, ed. Gerhard Müller (Berlin: de Gruyter, 1994), 746.

8 Edward Gibbon, *History of the Decline and Fall of the Roman Empire*, vol. 1 (London: Jones, 1826), 18.

9 James D. G. Dunn, *The Partings of the Ways: Between Christianity and Judaism and Their Significance for the Character of Christianity* (Philadelphia: Trinity International, 1991), 20.

10 Miskotte, *Biblical ABCs*, 39.

11 Maximus of Tyre, *Philosophical Orations*, 8:10, cited in Naomi Janowitz, *Icons of Power: Ritual Practices in Late Antiquity* (State College: Penn State Press, 2002), 38.

12 Jaś Elsner, *Imperial Rome and Christian Triumph: The Art of the Roman Empire AD 100–450* (Oxford: Oxford University Press, 1998), 154.

13 Smith, "Idolatry," 56.

14 Paul F. Knitter, preface to Hick and Knitter, *Myth of Christian Uniqueness*, viii.

15 D'Costa, *Christian Uniqueness Reconsidered*, ix.

16 Charles Taylor, "Inwardness and the Culture of Modernity," in *Zwischenbetrachtungen im Prozess der Aufklärung*, ed. A. Hönneth et al. (Frankfurt: Suhrkamp, 1989), 613.

17 See R. Kendall Soulen, "Cruising toward Bethlehem: Human Dignity and the New Eugenics," in *God and Human Dignity*, ed. Linda Woodhead and R. Kendall Soulen (Grand Rapids, MI: Eerdmans, 2006), 104–20.

18   See Muis, *Implicit Theology*, 169. Jan Muis draws attention in this connection to Eugene Rosenstock-Huessy's statement "und hinter seinem Namen treibt Gott sein Wesen nicht" (God does not assert his essence behind his name). With Muis and Rosenstock-Huessy, I think it is incorrect to separate the name YHWH as an immanent phenomenon from the expressly transcendent God. This is what Andrea D. Saner attempts to do in *"Too Much to Grasp": Exod 3:13–15 and the Reality of God* (Winona Lake, IN: Eisenbrauns, 2015). I agree with Saner that God is indeed "too much to grasp," but the cardinal sign of that truth is the Tetragrammaton itself, in comparison with which getting a handle on the anonymity of the unknowable God is child's play, as Gibbon pointed out long ago. Though outdated in certain respects, a valuable study of the interrelationship of the names of Exod 3:14–15 remains Oskar Grether, *Name und Wort Gotts in Alten Testament* (Giessen: Töpelmann, 1934).

19   Kierkegaard, *Sickness unto Death*, 33–34.

INDEX

SCRIPTURE INDEX